# EVERYTHING
# I
# EAT
## MAKES ME
# THIN

# EVERYTHING I EAT MAKES ME THIN

## Waking Up to Overeating Attitudes

### RICHARD CARLSON, Ph.D.

#### WITH

#### BARBARA CARLSON

**BANTAM BOOKS**
NEW YORK · TORONTO · LONDON · SYDNEY · AUCKLAND

*EVERYTHING I EAT MAKES ME THIN*
*A Bantam Book / February 1991*

*All rights reserved.*
*Copyright © 1991 by Richard Carlson, Ph.D.*
*Cover design copyright © 1991 by One Plus One Studio.*

*Library of Congress Cataloging-in-Publication Data*

Carlson, Richard, 1961–
   Everything I eat makes me thin : waking up to overeating attitudes
/ Richard Carlson, with Barbara Carlson.
     p.    cm.
   ISBN 0-553-35234-2
   1.  Obesity—Psychological aspects.    I.  Carlson, Barbara.
II. Title.
RC628.C38   1991
616.85'26—dc20
                                            90-39681
                                              CIP

*Published simultaneously in the United States and Canada*

---

*Bantam Books are published by Bantam Books, a division of Bantam*
*Doubleday Dell Publishing Group, Inc. Its trademark, consisting of the*
*words "Bantam Books" and the portrayal of a rooster, is Registered in*
*U.S. Patent and Trademark Office and in other countries. Marca Regis-*
*trada. Bantam Books, 666 Fifth Avenue, New York, New York 10103.*

---

# Contents

◆ v ◆

SECTION TWO

◆

# The Overeating Attitudes!

SECTION THREE

◆

# More "Food for Thought"

# ◆ Contents ◆

SECTION FOUR

◆

# Be Good to Yourself!

just like mom and dad."

The list of payoffs is unlimited and very different for everyone. The important point to remember

# INTRODUCTION: A PERSONAL STATEMENT

◆

I initially became interested in the impact attitudes and imagery have on healing while conducting a practice in the healing arts known as "Rolfing" and studying for my doctoral degree in psychology. I was fascinated by books written by such people as Norman Cousins *(Anatomy of an Illness)*, Louise L. Hay *(You Can Heal Your Life)*, Bernie Siegel, M.D. *(Love, Medicine, and Miracles)* and O. Carl Simonton, M.D. *(Getting Well Again)*. Each of these writers, all of whom contributed to my first book, *Healers on Healing* (with Benjamin Shield), emphasized the importance of attitudinal factors in the healing process.

I am a certified Rolfer and therapist with a doctoral degree in psychology. I maintain a private practice in the San Francisco Bay area where I work with people's bodies and help them with their body images. Rolfing is a type of body therapy that assists people to get in touch with and obtain the type of body and body image they would like to have. These goals are achieved through a combination of physical manipulations and mental imagery techniques.

Over the years I have observed that those patients who achieved a positive result in their bodies were invariably those who had first incorporated a positive mental outlook. By changing their thoughts, images, and attitudes about their bodies, these patients were able to alter their physiology and body structure in a beneficial way.

Because so many of my clients, as well as I myself (at the time), were overweight, I began to wonder if there might not also be a relationship between mental attitude and weight control. As I studied my clients, I quickly learned that, not only was there a relationship, but in fact attitude stood out as the *only* constant factor of success or failure in weight control. In other words, it didn't matter whether a client was on the Scarsdale Diet, the Pritikin, the Beverly Hills, the Fit-for-Life program, the Grapefruit Diet, or any other diet. In all the successful cases I observed, a positive attitude and view of self was the common element that determined people's success. Conversely, those who didn't, or couldn't, incorporate a new vision of themselves, and instead chose to rely solely on the components of the specific diet, were invariably disappointed. These people usually concluded that they had chosen the wrong diet, so they began searching for a better one.

Excited by my theory and observations, I decided to develop a set of techniques to promote a positive attitude for use in weight control. I was my own first guinea pig. By changing my attitudes about my body, I was able to drop from 213 to 185 pounds. Several years later, my weight remains steady.

The changed attitude I'm referring to is a whole new way of perceiving our bodies and our capacities. It involves a new way of looking at ourselves, as well as a series of mental exercises designed to alter our deepest belief systems, which so often prohibit us from achieving our goals.

This is not the first book on the importance of attitude, nor is it the first to point out that there is more to losing weight than choosing the right diet. This book does, however, offer a fresh and quite different perspective. It is my contention and experience that the specific diet you choose isn't even slightly relevant to your ultimate ability to lose weight. I have found, along with thousands of other unsuccessful dieters, that willpower and choosing the right diet provide a temporary cure at best. Almost always what is missing from a diet is the necessary body image and attitude for you to maintain the changes that come about from eating less. With these added components, which this book will provide, your body is able to function from a state of complete mental and subconscious health in reference to your weight.

The body, in its most natural state, can be viewed as a living and self-regulating machine. In this natural state, and left to its own devices, it will monitor and adjust its own weight very carefully and accurately. It is only through the interjection of harmful and negative perceptions (attitudes) that the body becomes confused and eventually loses its ability to self-regulate. A comparable analogy would be a computer system that works quite nicely until someone programs it to self-destruct.

Prior to the interjection of negative thoughts and images, which so many of us have about ourselves, the internal equilibrium and homeostasis capabilities of the human body are immense and impressive. The reason we overeat, or fail to stick to a diet is because our attitudes and self-perceptions fall away from this ideal state. The purpose of this book is to help bring back the attitudes and self-images that our bodies are intuitively most familiar with.

Overeaters Anonymous, one of the most life-changing weight loss and support programs ever created, recognizes the importance of turning over a problem to a "higher power." In fact one of OA's major principles or "steps" reads, "I came to realize that a power greater than myself is the only solution." While different people and systems refer to their "higher self" by different names, this book refers to it as the "subconscious mind." This higher (or subconscious) part of ourselves ultimately dictates our behavior. This is where our most deeply held beliefs and attitudes about ourselves come from and where they continue to exist.

Our subconscious minds can be our very best friends or our own worst enemies. For most people, the distribution between these two extremes remains random. In other words, the subconscious is a part of the mind over which most of us have little or no control. There are times when our subconscious minds work to help us, and there are times when they can almost literally tear us apart.

We can learn to utilize and control our subconscious minds through an understanding of some basic principles, a little practice, and a few psychological insights about ourselves. As I mentioned above, I have discovered that individuals who are successful in their weight loss attempts tend to look at themselves in a positive manner. I am not the discoverer of this information; I am merely passing on what I have seen work in so many people's lives so that readers of this book can benefit from the attitudinal perspectives that have worked and continue to work for others. This book is a compilation of the principles and knowledge necessary to begin to communicate with the subconscious mind as the helpful and supportive friend it can be.

My co-author, Barbara Carlson, is a living example of the potential of attitudinal living. Her physical fitness, as well as her skills in the use of positive affirmations, imagination, and guided imagery are something to behold. After mastering the techniques herself, Barbara utilized the exercises and attitudes expressed in this book to become one of the top masters (over 40) marathon (26.2 miles) runners in the United States! Barbara, who also teaches the techniques described in this book in her own private practice, claims that "attitude" and "inner work" are responsible for both her physical fitness and athletic success.

There are many fine books and qualified experts on dieting and nutrition, and a great many people buying these books and listening to the experts; yet very few come away having lost their excess weight. Even fewer are able to keep it off. Why? Unlike some advocates of attitudinal approaches, I recognize that experts on nutrition and diet can be helpful. In fact, I am grateful they exist because people have diverse nutritional needs. Experts on diet, however, shouldn't be considered the ticket to permanent weight loss. Rather, the common denominator of dietary success or failure is your "attitude" about yourself and your diet, whatever it may be. After mastering this, the most important element of weight loss, you can then choose the diet you prefer.

This book provides not only effective techniques but also the psychological insights necessary to support the changes you will be making. I work with people and their bodies every day. I see what works for them and what doesn't. The success rate of people who use the techniques and knowledge you are about to learn is astounding. There's no question that your body's physiology is affected by the thoughts, attitudes, and images you put into it. This is not the first book that utilizes affirmations and inner work to achieve sustained weight loss; it certainly won't be the last. More and more people are becoming familiar with these types of techniques and especially why the techniques are so powerful. I practice and teach the use of affirmations, visualization, guided imagery, and meditation so I know the techniques and information are effective. I know they can work for you!

Richard Carlson, Ph.D.

# The Essentials
of
Inner Work

# 1

## The Past Is Over
### . . . Or Is It?

Spiritual practices and psychological schools of thought from around the world teach us the importance of "living in the present moment." Why is this teaching so important? Even more perplexing is the question, "Why is this so difficult?"

From generation to generation, each of us has been taught that the *past predicts the future.* A person who is psychologically sound and of good judgment is seen to look carefully to the past when thinking of future plans. So ingrained is our attachment to our past that we believe our future is beyond our control.

The belief that our past predicts our future is very harmful indeed. It encourages us to think about our future and expect it to be like the past. It leaves little room for growth or change because we see ourselves as "victims" whose lives are predestined to duplicate and repeat our past actions, behavior, and circumstances. Since we believe that the past repeats itself, we must forgive, and completely leave our past behind.

The purpose of this book is to help you discover that *what you were is not what you have to be today*. Although this principle can apply to all aspects of your life, we will be applying it to the topic of weight control. Everything you will be reading and each of the exercises you will be practicing are geared toward freeing you from your past belief systems about your eating and your weight, thus enabling you to form new ones. It is only through "letting go" of your past that you can look to the future in a practical and realistic manner. As you begin to do so, you will be beginning to "live in the present," rather than in the past.

As you will see throughout this book, your beliefs about yourself were formed in essentially three ways. The first way you learned about "who you were" was by listening to the significant people in your childhood. For most of us, our significant people consisted primarily of our parents, although siblings, relatives, and others can certainly play important roles as well.

We learned, very early on, exactly what our parents thought about our eating habits and about food in general. We learned the importance that food played in our parents' lives. It turns out that most people who go through life with weight issues had parents who reinforced to them how important it was to eat. In addition, those people were often told what "good children" they were for eating large amounts of food and finishing everything on their plates. Many times, as children, we received the most positive attention while sitting in our high chairs playing with and eating our food. Very simply, we learned to associate food with good times, positive reinforcement, and love.

As we developed into adults, each of us carried with us certain labels and beliefs about ourselves, which were grounded and formulated in our childhood. Some of the more popular messages people remember, revolving around the issue of food, are, "You have such a big appetite," "You're so cute and chubby," and, "You're such a good girl for eating all your food; Mommy and Daddy love you when you eat it all up." As we develop into adults, we actually believe that we are people who have big appetites. We believe that it's just the way we are, and there's nothing we can do to change.

The second way we developed our "belief systems" was by making choices in our lives that reinforced the labels we were learning about ourselves. This was an easy way to avoid disappointing those people we loved most in the world. For example, we would choose to eat, even after feeling full, in an attempt to please Mother and Dad. We learned that eating was an effective and easy way to gain their approval. These types of reinforcing choices were made on a daily basis until they became an integral part of our lives. Today, twenty, thirty, even fifty years later, we are making the same types of choices without the rewards we once received.

The final way we developed our beliefs about ourselves was through the messages, both verbal and mental, that we fed (and continue to feed) ourselves on a daily basis. This is the most important of the three elements involved in formulating our belief systems because it is reinforced dozens of times per day. We give ourselves many daily messages that dictate our behavior and actions, including what, and how much, we choose to eat.

Messages can also be called *affirmations*. Their purpose is to validate what we perceive to be "truth" and "reality." For example, a message you might already give to yourself is, *I have a big appetite.* There are several reasons for giving yourself such a message. First, as we have already seen, you may have received this label early in childhood, reinforced hundreds or even thousands of times by your parents, brothers and sisters, and other family members. Second, in an attempt to keep your parents' approval, as you got older, you made choices in your life that reinforced your label. You probably maintained a large appetite, thus reinforcing what you had learned about yourself. Finally, you heard the message so many times that you actually adopted it as part of your personality and vocabulary. It became so much a part of you that you began giving *yourself* the message. This is the point where the trouble really starts. Once you begin giving yourself a learned message, it implies that you then accept the message as *absolute truth*. Today, then, when you think of yourself, you think of a person "with a big appetite." Whenever the situation arises, whether you are by yourself or with others, you reinforce the message by telling yourself, or someone else, what a large appetite you have. As the years go by, the message becomes more and more a part of you until you can think of yourself in no other way. Because you now believe so strongly in your "large appetite," you actually feel the need (unconsciously) to find ways to maintain it.

In addition to discovering how your eating patterns and belief systems began, it's also important to understand the "psychological payoffs" involved in maintaining them. Psychological payoffs are like stock-market dividends, except that their value is false. They are temporary rewards that subconsciously encourage us to maintain the "status quo." While we each have developed our own psychological payoffs for maintaining our weight problem, here are just a few to consider:

1. A weight problem can help keep us safe from intimacy or close relationships.
2. Overeating can satisfy an unconscious desire to please our parents.

3. We can use a weight problem to justify our overall poor self-image.
4. We can tell ourselves, and others, that life is harder for us than it is for others because we are overweight.
5. We can justify laziness, lack of activity, or lack of exercise because we "aren't in shape."
6. We can use being overweight as an excuse to not do certain things that we find unpleasant, that we might otherwise "have to do."
7. If one or both of our parents are overweight, we can unconsciously believe that we are "just like mom and dad."

The list of payoffs is unlimited and very different for everyone. The important point to remember is that there are many psychological reasons, both conscious and unconscious, why people find it difficult to maintain, or drop to, an optimal weight. As you continue to read through this book, see if you can think of some of the "payoffs" you personally may have adopted.

Because our belief systems are so thoroughly ingrained in our thought processes, and oftentimes are completely blocked from our awareness, we *must* tackle the problem with methods that are both supportive of change and capable of penetrating our subconscious minds. (The next few chapters will explain this and other terms you need to understand to get the most out of this book.)

"Affirmations" are one of the tools in this book which you will learn to utilize. They have proved to be an extremely effective method for altering our existing belief systems. Affirmations both get us in touch with the way we communicate with ourselves, and teach us new, more productive alternatives. In addition, they give us a sense of what we expect from ourselves—how capable we perceive ourselves to be. In a sense, they can be seen as appropriate and effective means to *update* our current belief systems about ourselves. As our belief systems and our personal "truths" are updated to represent today's reality, we will become capable of living fully in the "present moment," rather than being victimized by our past. In addition to the affirmations, each chapter will include a discussion of the reasons a particular "overeating attitude" developed, along with examples for illustration, and specific exercises to practice.

This moment is the only one you have. Every moment then, can be seen as a new opportunity to change your current perspective and corresponding set of beliefs about your life. As you read through this book, remember that the past is over. What you are offered here is an opportunity to begin again with fresh choices that will determine your future. Chapter 2 will go into greater detail about what affirmations and inner work are all about and how they can be helpful to you.

# 2

◆ ═══════ ◆

# What I Say Is What I Get

◆

Everything we learn in our lives is a *direct* result of something we have been told—everything! All of us can think of areas where we were told we were "no good," "inadequate," or "clumsy." Similarly, all of us wish that our parents had given us either more credit or less criticism in certain areas of our upbringing. I've never met a single person who felt he/she had received too much positive praise.

Taking it to an extreme, imagine for a moment that you grew up in a household where you were *never once* given a compliment, appropriate credit, praise, recognition, or even a pat on the back. Everything that was said around the house was negative and no one was allowed *any* positive feedback, no matter what the circumstances! Under these conditions, what do you think you'd be like today? It's pretty frightening, isn't it?

We all know that what a child thinks about herself will affect, if not determine, how well she will do in school, how well she will be able to make friends, and especially, how happy she will be. With all this proven and easily understandable knowledge, why do we continue torturing ourselves with the same types of patterns? It's almost as though we feel we deserve to be treated with disrespect and lack of love.

This book is about relearning how to talk to yourself. In doing so, you can achieve the respect and self-love you've always wanted and needed. The key to this "relearning" lies in the understanding and correct use of what are called "affirmations."

An affirmation is defined as a positive assertion. More specifically, it is a word, or series of words, either written or spoken, that we repeat to ourselves. Affirmations can be seen as instructions to our bodies. They are messages, or commands, that let our bodies know how we wish them to behave. Affirmations are based on the premise that our words and thoughts have a tremendous amount of power and influence to them—so much power and influence, in fact, that virtually everything we say or think to ourselves, either positive or negative, will come back to either help us or get in our way. Affirmations assume that our minds are unable to implement *any* new belief or attitude as long as our conversations continue to deny them. In other words, it can be said that *What we say is what we get!* The more frequently we repeat affirmations and the more certainty and meaning we put into them, the more influence and power they will have.

Unfortunately, for most of us, our affirmations are primarily unconscious in nature. In other words, we repeat to ourselves words or phrases out of pure habit rather than from conscious choice. We give ourselves dozens of negative messages every day, never realizing that we are forming our view of ourselves based on our words and thoughts. As we will see, our view of ourselves ultimately determines our ability to lose weight.

Our subconscious is part of our mind, but it is not immediately available to our awareness. In other words, it is the part of us that controls our actions even though we are not aware of it. Our subconscious mind is very much like a sponge. It listens to, and soaks up, our words, which define and shape the way we see ourselves and our world. For the most part, subconscious minds are without judgment or preference. They don't know, or care to distinguish, right from wrong, positive from negative, or good from bad. The only skill they have is a keen ability to "listen" so they will know exactly what action to take. In a sense, they are trained to take "orders" from our spoken words. As our subconscious minds listen to our words, they try to validate and make true whatever we say or think about.

Your subconscious mind wants to be "right" as often as it can. It wants to prove everything that you say to yourself, regardless of whether or not the message is positive or negative. For example, if you say to yourself, or to someone else, "I can't stop myself from eating," your subconscious mind feels as though it is actually doing you a favor by attempting to validate your statement. It will look for validation of your statements in any way that it can. If you tell yourself "I can't stop myself from eating," your subconscious mind will remind you of this fact every time you eat a meal. It will say, "See, I told you. You never did have any willpower. See how you're eating again?" It will tell you this even if what you're eating is on your diet plan. The subconscious mind is looking for validation of your spoken words, not for how well you're doing on your diet. If you are giving yourself negative messages about your eating habits, it is not only possible but, in fact, probable that your subconscious mind has no idea that you even have the desire to lose weight! You may believe that you want to lose weight; you may even be obsessed about it. In actuality, however, you may be telling your subconscious mind exactly the opposite. You may be suggesting, through unconscious affirmations, not only that you *don't want to lose weight* but that, even if you did, *you would be incapable of it.* This is a very important realization for successful weight loss because awareness of your present affirmation patterns can free you from your past belief systems and pave the way to a new type of freedom.

The subconscious mind has *nothing* else to do but to wait for your instructions. With this in mind, you can see that it's extremely important to minimize, and eventually eliminate, the number of times you verbalize any type of negative message. Statements such as, "I'll never be able to lose weight," or "losing weight is a very hard thing to do," simply impregnate your subconscious mind with negative thought forms, thereby blocking your internal wisdom and bringing additional limitation into your life.

In a sense, *everything* we say to ourselves is an affirmation of some kind. This is because each time we speak we are communicating with our "sponge-like" subconscious minds in one way or another. Negative statements like "I can't stop myself from overeating," or "every time I eat cheese I gain weight," are affirmations, just as positive statements such as "I love to exercise," or "I only eat when I'm hungry." These are the types of messages given to our subconscious minds that will determine how our bodies will behave. If we believe, and continue to tell ourselves, "I can't stop myself from eating," the following process will occur in our subconscious: First, our words will be registered in the subconscious mind for processing. The mind will recognize that we have given attention to the fact that we "can't stop eating." Since the subconscious is now focusing on "eating," it begins reminding our bodies of our *self-induced* limitation that both eating and our weight are beyond our control. In a sense, then, our subconscious mind is telling our body that (1) we *must* eat, even if we are not hungry, and (2) we must respond to our eating by gaining weight.

As already mentioned, our affirmations are received as "orders" by our subconscious mind. Our words are like an army "General" giving the orders, while our subconscious mind acts as the "Private" who is trained *only* to listen and respond to what he or she is told. Our General demands that our Private comply with his wishes, whatever they may be. Our Private, out of his sense of helplessness and his attempt to be a good soldier, does whatever is necessary to find a way to obey. He will do things like go to the refrigerator, even when he's not hungry, to get something to eat. He will do anything he can to follow the order given by the General which is essentially, **"YOU CAN'T STOP YOURSELF FROM OVEREATING."** His response is always, **"YES, SIR!"**

Fortunately, the subconscious mind is absolutely consistent with its habits. If you change the emphasis of your statements, or "orders," from negative to positive, the subconscious will put an equal amount of effort into making itself "right." It will fight like mad to validate whatever you have said.

Thus, if you begin to tell yourself that **"I only eat when I'm hungry,"** the mind will immediately begin to follow your new set of orders. With enough practice, the mind and the body will begin to believe that you only eat when you're hungry. Your subconscious will look for validation of your positive statements in exactly the same way it did for the negative ones. For example, if you tell yourself that you only eat when you're hungry, your subconscious will remind you frequently throughout the day that this is true. It will say to you, "See, you didn't eat again. I knew you didn't eat when you weren't hungry. Good for you." Each time you repeat the affirmation, you will be reinforcing the fact that you are in complete control of your eating habits.

It has been my experience that the body follows the mind's instructions to a "T." If the body is told, "When I eat this food I will gain weight," the body begins the process of following instructions. It is my belief that one of the primary reasons diets don't usually work is because so many negative thoughts and discussions go along with them. Dieters are notorious for telling themselves, and others, over and over again, how much weight they are going to gain by eating certain foods. It's amazing to listen to people talking in restaurants. I'd estimate that close to 50 percent of the table conversations I've heard in recent years are focused, at least in part, on "how fattening the food is," or "how much I'm overeating," or "how difficult it's going to be to lose the weight I'm going to gain from this meal." It's all so ridiculous because it does no good! As we will see in a later chapter, all self-criticism is essentially a complete waste of time and is very counterproductive to weight loss. Eventually, when dieters do break down and eat some of the food they have been talking about, their bodies respond in the only way they know how: namely by doing exactly what they have always been told, gaining weight. What option do they have? All they have *ever* been told is that they will overeat and that they will surely gain weight because of it. As they gain weight, the subconscious mind is pleased, because once again it has been reinforced that it is doing its job—and doing it well!

Dieters compound their problem by telling themselves over and over again how "hard" it is to diet. Think about it for a moment. What kinds of negative messages do you give to yourself when you are attempting to diet? Have you ever told yourself how difficult it is to diet or how much work it is going to be to lose weight? What about how "boring it is to exercise," or how little time you have for the same? Each of these statements, and so many others like them, contain instructions to the subconscious mind that may as well be translated as follows: **"I CAN'T LOSE WEIGHT."** Not only do these types of statements do nothing to help but, in fact, they are quite counterproductive.

I would like to suggest that, from this point

forth, you have the power within yourself to choose which types of messages you are going to focus your attention on, and what is going to happen to your body as a result. You alone need to decide what types of messages you want to send to your mind and body.

Everywhere you go, you will hear people telling you all the reasons why "it's difficult to lose weight," that "only willpower will do the trick," and that "you should never eat pizza." You need to make a *conscious* choice to decide upon your own affirmations. If you don't, you can bet that society, friends, spouses, neighbors, relatives, and advertisers will try to decide for you. If you let them, you can bet that they will decide on the belief system of difficulty, willpower, hard work, and failure. Wouldn't you rather decide for yourself, not only what you are going to eat, but when, how much, and especially what will happen as a result?

Affirmations are learned in steps. It's often the case that for the first few days, or practice sessions, individuals feel as though they are tricking or misrepresenting the truth to themselves as they give themselves positive suggestions for the very first time. This is *only* because we are unfamiliar and uncomfortable with giving ourselves positive messages. Most of us are so accustomed to negative reinforcement that positive suggestion takes some getting used to. No need to worry, however! Very shortly, you will retrain yourself to accept positive suggestions in exactly the same fashion as you have always received negative ones. In fact, someday you will wonder how you could have ever given yourself negative messages. You will ask yourself, "What good can it possibly do to berate myself with negative comments, which only suggest that I'm incapable of change?" I'm convinced that, after learning the art of effective affirmations, along with practicing the exercises contained in this book, you will see for yourself how easy it can be to take control of your weight, based on the messages you give to yourself.

```
E X E R C I S E
2A
```

## Avoiding
## Self-Criticism

Many people have trouble believing that it could possibly be a difficult task simply to avoid criticizing oneself for an extended period of time. This is because most people believe they are totally conscious of everything they say and do. Because the message of this book is based on the idea that we are constantly bombarding ourselves with negative talk and self-criticism, it's very important to get a feeling of the extent to which this is true. This exercise is designed to demonstrate how surprisingly difficult it is to speak to oneself "only" in a positive way.

Start with a period of 24 hours. Tell three or four people the purpose of this exercise. Perhaps you can choose a family member at home and a few close friends or associates at work. Whomever you choose, let them know that their job is to keep an eye on you! Also, keep a pen and a pad of paper with you at all times during the day.

The purpose of this exercise is to avoid any self-criticism for the 24-hour period. This includes "constructive" criticism as well as any other kind. You are allowed no "harmless" comments or even jokes about yourself that suggest you are anything but okay just as you are. No "I'm overweight," or "I'm clumsy," or "I can't help it," or "Silly me," or "I've always been that way," or "I'll probably have a bad day," or "I've never been any good at that," or any other statement that suggests that there is some way in which you need to improve.

Any time you, or your helpers, catch you offering criticism to yourself, write the nature of the criticism on your pad of paper. Keep track, and you'll be surprised at how often you're tempted!

# 3

# The Nuts and Bolts
# of Affirmations

All positive affirmations are effective as a means toward altering negative attitudes and/or toward changing a pattern of behavior. Any time you either consciously or unconsciously give yourself positive feedback, or life-enhancing messages, you are in effect replacing negative belief systems with new, more productive ones. When working with affirmations, there are no hard and fast rules or procedures to follow that will make or break your success. Nevertheless, there are a few important tips to keep in mind, which can make your affirmations even more productive than they might otherwise be.

Affirmations can be practiced in essentially two

ways. I recommend that both methods be used on a daily basis until you find the routine that works best for you. I call the first method a "practice period." This is where you actually sit or lie down, with the sole intent of practicing your affirmations. Generally, effective practice periods last between five and ten minutes and should be done twice daily. For most people, the best times to practice are first thing in the morning and as close to bedtime as possible. The number of times per day and the amount of time spent, however, are entirely up to you. Choose whatever time schedule you are most comfortable with. If you plan on practicing only once per day, it is generally most effective to do so right before going to sleep. When practiced at this time, affirmations are easily remembered by the subconscious mind and help ingrain the messages into your consciousness throughout the night.

I call the second type of practice, "active affirmations." These types of affirmations are practiced throughout the day and become a normal and integral part of your daily life. There is no set or planned time to practice these affirmations because they are spontaneous in nature: You simply practice them as they come to your mind. The more time you spend in your practice periods, the more frequently "active affirmations" will present themselves to you.

Any affirmation can be practiced in either of the above two methods. For example, let's suppose you were using the affirmation, **"I ONLY EAT**

**WHEN I'M HUNGRY."** If you were in a practice period, you would be sitting or lying down with your eyes closed. You would be in a very relaxed state, taking several deep breaths, and clearing your mind of any external distractions. As you became very relaxed, you would repeat the message to yourself over and over again. You would be replacing your existing beliefs about your eating habits with this very simple, straightforward message.

If you were using the "active" method, the procedure would be slightly different, primarily depending on your physical setting. Instead of having your eyes closed while lying in a comfortable position, for example, you might be on your way to a restaurant, or driving home from work. You can be virtually anywhere while practicing active affirmations and the time you do them is up to you. Whenever an affirmation comes to mind is the right time to practice. For example, using the situation above, you might think of the affirmation while walking into your favorite restaurant. As you were being seated, you would repeat to yourself, **"I ONLY EAT WHEN I'M HUNGRY"** over and over again. This affirmation would be sending a message to your subconscious mind about your eating habits, thus dictating your behavior and allowing you to eat less.

One of the first things to remember about affirmations is that they are **fun and easy.** This is important to recognize because many of us are taught that, for something to be successful, it must also be hard. The reason affirmations are so simple is because they are not learned from the intellect. In fact, they represent an opportunity to move away from our logical, thinking mind and into the world of intuition, creativity, and higher knowledge.

Affirmations are most effective when both the body and the mind are in a very relaxed state. Before beginning (assuming you are using the practice method) find a comfortable, quiet, and relaxing place. Next, take several very deep breaths. As you close your eyes and begin to feel a deep sense of relaxation, picture in your mind either the words or the images you are attempting to convey to your subconscious mind.

The greatest successes will come to you as more and more of your visual images include *only* positive pictures. Your subconscious mind will help your body create slimness, as you replace your existing self-image, which may include negative pictures, with your new one, which will include only slimness, health, beauty, and love. For the purposes of weight control, your new self-image involves seeing yourself as already slim. This means that you are already trim and fit; *not* that someday you are going to be. More specifically, in terms of affirmations, it's the difference between "I am going to have a slim body," and "I have a slim body now!" Whenever possible, use the present tense, or "I have a slim body NOW."

A good rule of thumb to keep in mind is to

practice affirming what you *do* want, not what you don't. In this sense, affirmations become less effective when we use the word, "NOT." For example, the affirmation "I will *not* eat ice cream," isn't nearly as effective as it could be. The word "not" tends to put even greater emphasis and attention on what it is you are attempting to avoid. In this instance, it's putting more attention on "ice cream," thus, it is possible that the affirmation can actually encourage you to eat it. A more productive and positive way of giving yourself the message that you don't wish to eat ice cream (or anything else) would be to say "I enjoy only healthy food that nourishes my body."

It's important to note, as we relearn how to talk to ourselves, that the subconscious mind does not understand jokes! Many of us are used to making "harmless" jokes about ourselves such as "Oh, I'm just a blimp," or "I might as well eat it because I'm already fat as a cow." Whether or not we're "kidding," doesn't matter in the least to the subconscious mind, which simply registers what we say and tries to validate it. Whatever we say to ourselves is registered as a picture in our mind. If we tell ourselves, joking or not, that we are "fat as a cow," our subconscious mind begins the process of formulating a picture of what we have just said. Once the picture is clear, the subconscious mind does what it can to make the statement true. It might convince us to overeat, slow down our metabolism, or any number of other destructive tricks, all designed to sabotage our success. It will do whatever it has to, to help us make true what we have just said.

With this in mind, you can see how important your words can be. Fortunately, positive words and thoughts have exactly as much effect as negative ones. The more you tell yourself that "I only eat when I'm hungry," or any other positive message, the more your subconscious mind will believe you. Each time the affirmation is repeated, the subconscious mind will do what it can to help validate the statement. Eventually, the idea that you only eat when you're hungry will become a new attitude, which will replace the "overeating attitude" that "I have no control over how much I eat." The new attitude will be such a part of your life that you won't even need to think about it; you simply won't eat unless you're hungry!

Another important factor of success is repetition. The more you repeat a positive message to yourself, the more you are impressing upon your subconscious mind the valuable message you are giving it. Even if you need to repeat a certain affirmation one hundred times a day for a month, you can never overdo it! Many of us have told ourselves thousands and thousands of times throughout our lives the same worn-out negative messages. Since we have also heard the negative messages from others, is it any wonder we tend to believe them? The only way to change our current perspectives and corresponding set of beliefs is to change the types of messages we give to ourselves. The more ingrained the messages are, the more repetition is required to change them.

Enthusiasm is another key to success with affirmations. How much more effective do you become when you are enthusiastic about something? Obviously when you are excited about a topic, it's easier and more fun to find a way to create success. When repeating the message **"I love healthy food"** to yourself, try saying it like it really matters to you. Go ahead and give this affirmation a try!

---

## I LOVE HEALTHY FOOD!!!!!!!!

---

No one is going to hear you or object to your enthusiasm. You are attempting to develop a new "attitude" about food which is tremendously important. The more meaning you put into your words, the more your subconscious mind is going to be certain of the message it is receiving.

Affirmations can be practiced in many ways. In fact, the more the merrier! It can be tremendously effective to reinforce your verbal affirmations by writing them down. As you write down the message you wish to receive, think very carefully about the words you are writing. The act of writing something down allows your mind to focus even more on what you are thinking. This allows your subconcious mind another opportunity to "let in" the desired message. In addition, you can repeat your affirmations out loud, to yourself or to others. You can incorporate them into a song, a meditation, a prayer, or a chant. Any methods that work for you are the ones to use.

Finally, believe in the new messages you are giving yourself and believe in your ability to implement positive change. The subconscious mind is perhaps the most powerful tool any of us have been given. We now have the power, knowledge, and ability to utilize this remarkable tool to its maximum efficiency. Believe in yourself!

While this chapter has dealt specifically with the use of affirmations, keep in mind that affirmations are only one type of "inner work." The exercises at the end of each chapter are an important part of utilizing the affirmations to their fullest extent and training your subconscious mind to accept your new eating "attitudes." The exercises are geared toward the specific chapter they follow and are divided into the categories of mental exercises, guided visualizations, simple meditations, drawings, and philosophic food for thought.

## EXERCISE

## 3A:

### Creating a Self-Talk Tape

An extremely effective way to maximize your efficiency in affirmation work is to create a "self-talk tape." Listening to your own voice practicing specific affirmations on a tape is a very powerful tool for change. It is a way of speaking to you, and recalling your goals, in a direct and efficient way. As you repeatedly listen to your tape, you are reinforcing the types of positive messages that you have chosen to affirm. As with all types of affirmations, listening to yourself in a positive way can change negative perceptions you have about yourself into positive ones.

The following is a list of ten steps that will help you create a useful and creative self-talk tape. These steps, like any type of inner work, should be viewed as guidelines, not mandates.

**(1)** It is best to purchase a 30-minute endless loop tape. This way the messages can continue repeating themselves until you decide to turn them off.

**(2)** Create a specific list of affirmations that you want to tell yourself. List them in an order that makes sense to you.

**(3)** While creating a tape, it is helpful to use *your* name within the statements. For example, "I, Richard, love to take care of myself."

**(4)** Use the present tense for maximum results. For example, "I love to eat healthy food," rather than "I am going to eat healthy food."

**(5)** Use only positive words and phrases.

**(6)** Get right to the point.

**(7)** Believe in your heart that what you are hearing is the truth.

**(8)** Record the messages onto your tape as many times as necessary in order to have it sound just the way you like it. You want the messages to sound positive and self-assured.

**(9)** This exercise should be a lot of fun and should feel good! Be sensitive to the way you feel when you're listening to your words.

**(10)** Wait until you finish reading this book before attempting to make your tape. The information you will read will be helpful in creating just the right tape.

# 4

♦ ══════ ♦

# Visualization

♦

One of the most important aspects to success-ful inner work is the ability to picture your-self, in your own mind, as you would like to be. In other words, really "seeing" your affirmation as a present reality is a major key to success. This ability to see yourself, or your affirmation, is called "visu-alization." Because this is such an essential part of effective affirmations, this chapter is devoted to this very important skill.

Visualization is important from two perspec-tives. First, it's a key to really "owning" your affir-mations. It's important to see the words in your mind as you are saying them. Secondly, visualiza-tion can be used independently of (and in addition to) pure affirmations. In this sense, then, it is both an integral part of affirmations and an independent element of inner work. The difference between affirmations and visualization is simply that visualization, unlike affirmations, doesn't need words to be effective. You can visualize not only spoken affirmations, such as **"I look at my body with respect and love,"** but also visual images, such as seeing yourself as a thin, beautiful, and healthy person. You can simply close your eyes and picture yourself as the person you wish to be, no words required! Toward the end of this chapter I have provided two nonverbal exercises to give you an opportunity to see and practice what a "visualization" exercise is all about. As you practice your affirmations, you will find that visual imagery, or "visualization," is a wonderful aspect to inner work. In some instances people find that visualizations are even more effective than verbal affirmations. Both spoken affirmations and visual imagery are tremendously effective and can be practiced together or independently with great success.

Perhaps the most exciting area in which visualization has recently become popular is in the area of traditional medicine and surgery. Thousands of physicians from around the world now use visualization routinely in their daily practices. Visualization can be, and has been, used for everything from reducing a simple headache to the elimination of usually fatal diseases. Dr. Bernie Siegel, founder of the Exceptional Cancer Patients Program in New Haven, Connecticut, and best-selling author of the beautiful book, *Love, Medicine, and Miracles,* describes many documented cases where visualization has not only prolonged life but also, in some instances, helped to completely eliminate cancerous tumors. In addition, Dr. O. Carl Simonton, another pioneer in the use of visualization and co-author of the popular book, *Getting Well Again,* routinely teaches both physicians and patients the usefulness and skill of visualization in the treatment of cancer. Because of the pronounced effect that images in the mind can have on the body, visualization yields a tremendous amount of power in virtually any aspect of life. If doctors can teach patients to use visualization to aid them in eliminating cancer and other life-threatening diseases from their bodies, we can certainly do the same to eliminate fat and excess weight!

Anything that happens in life is a direct result of a thought. In other words, a thought or idea *always* precedes the creation of anything. For example, if you wish to design and create a beautiful garden in your backyard, you must first create a picture in your mind of what you want the garden to look like. Similarly, when you want to lose weight, it's tremendously important to be able to "visualize" exactly what it is you hope to accomplish: how much weight you'd like to lose, and what you'll look like when you reach your goal. With visualization, we are formulating our specific goal inside our own minds. Once our vision is clear, our bodies will then know how to respond. Without a very clear goal however, it's very difficult to get to where we want to go.

Most people believe that willpower and hard work are the only viable ways to achieve results in weight loss. Unfortunately, however, these people disregard the *single most important part* of the process: "seeing" themselves as thin people. Virtually all people who successfully lose weight had to picture themselves first as being thin. If you can't see yourself as succeeding, how then will you do it? If you picture your garden as a sloppy mess, how in the world will you ever create a masterpiece? In actuality, it would be very tricky. The same is true with weight loss. As soon as you are able to see yourself as thin (and being the weight you wish to be) you have opened the door for your body to respond. Unfortunately, if you close your eyes and picture yourself as overweight, that is how you will tend to remain because that is the weight your body has determined you wish it to be. However, if you are able to picture yourself as fit, healthy, and thin, then your body will receive the visual message that change (lesser weight) is now an acceptable alternative.

Visualization is one of the critical elements to successful weight loss. You may lose some weight by dieting alone, but the results will probably be temporary. As long as the subconscious mind sees you as overweight, your body will perceive any weight loss as a mistake in the body's equilibrium and optimal state. Your body will feel the need to adjust to what it perceives to be a more appropriate weight.

Most people believe that they are overweight due to their tendency to overeat. While this is true, it's even more important to recognize and change the "overeating attitude" that is causing the overeating in the first place; seeing oneself as an overweight person is the attitude in need of change. The reason people are overweight is because, at some level, they see themselves (and think of themselves) as overweight. This vision of themselves may be conscious or unconscious; either way, it needs to be changed.

We have many unconscious beliefs about ourselves, which developed in early childhood. These beliefs are reinforced so frequently that they become a part of our consciousness. Once we accept them as absolute truth, they become an "attitude" about ourselves, or in this instance, an "overeating attitude." The realization of why you are overweight helps break the pattern of weight gain. Your body responds to the way you perceive it to be. It will tend to maintain the exact weight, shape, and level of fitness that your personal image and subconscious mind allow.

Although there are many important aspects to result-producing visualizations, three points stick out as being particularly relevant for the purposes of this book. These are clarity, belief in your vision, and repetition.

Clarity means vividly picturing yourself as the

person you wish to be. It means staying with your visualization for long periods of time, if necessary, in order to become the person you are visualizing. You have the ability to see in your mind anything you wish to see. If you find it difficult to focus your attention or create visual images, simply be aware that visualization, like everything else, takes some practice to master. Never tell yourself you aren't doing well enough. You are doing fine! As you continue to practice, your visions will become clearer and clearer. Eventually, it will be like watching a movie in your mind. It takes a little time to learn to fine-tune the clarity of the picture. The beauty of the process is that you write the script as you want it to be, in addition to playing the leading role.

Belief means trusting in yourself. Know that your visualizations are effective and are working for you at their own pace. Trust that the visions in your mind are exactly the right ones to help you lose weight. Remind yourself that every successful venture requires a belief on the part of the participant. Everything is more difficult, if not impossible, before we believe in ourselves. Think about all the times you were attempting something new. Remember how much easier it felt once you allowed yourself to think that you just might be able to do it.

Repetition speaks for itself. Make your visualizations and affirmations a regular and important part of your life. Just as with driving a car, the more practice you get, the more comfortable you become.

Similarly, the more you practice a particular visualization, the more ingrained it will become in your subconscious mind. Eventually, with enough practice, your visualizations, whatever form they take, will allow you to form new "attitudes" about yourself, thus replacing any remaining "overeating attitudes." Your new image of yourself will become second nature and will be seen as "just the way you are."

**EXERCISE**

# 4A

Although the procedure for using visualization is quite simple, the results are extremely powerful. At this point, let's take a few moments to practice a couple of visualization exercises. The first exercise is geared toward obtaining a flatter stomach and waistline, while the second helps you determine your "ideal body image." These types of exercises can be done in several ways. If you wish to practice alone, one effective method is to read the exercise into a tape recorder and listen to your own words, as discussed in Exercise 3A, "Creating a Self-Talk Tape." If you'd rather practice the exercise without a tape recorder, simply read through the exercise several times in advance, then lead yourself through from memory. If you have a friend you'd like to work with, this can be very helpful. You can take turns leading each other through the procedure. I encourage you to try each of the methods and see which is most effective for you. For now, let's begin.

After selecting the goal you wish to achieve (in this example a slimmer belly), close your eyes and allow yourself to relax. After taking a few very deep, slow breaths, begin to feel yourself sinking into your chair. As you relax, begin to form a picture in your mind of the goal you wish to create. Since you wish to have a flatter stomach, picture yourself in exactly the way you wish to be. See your stomach muscles and thin waistline on your perfectly formed body. See the exact shape of your hips and abdomen. Imagine as many details of yourself as you possibly can. Imagine not only your flat, firm stomach but also all the other parts of your body. In addition, picture your surroundings, what you are wearing (if anything), and whom you are with (if anyone).

Remember that you are not picturing someone else as being thin, but rather yourself. In other words, you are actually becoming the visualization. As you see yourself as the person you wish to be, imagine also the feelings associated with your body.

Notice how your thinner body experiences a great deal of vitality and energy. Take great pride in your beautiful body. It serves you well and deserves a great deal of attention and love. Before you open your eyes, thank yourself for being such a receptive and gracious person. Thank yourself for eating all the right foods that enabled you to obtain and keep your beautiful physique. One last time before opening your eyes, picture your thin waistline and the firm surrounding muscles. Know that you are on your way to creating the body you have always dreamed of. Open your eyes and notice how you feel. Now thank yourself for the way you are right now. Know that, even though you are losing weight and developing a firmer, healthier body, you are wonderful and okay just the way you are. As we will see later, this last point is critical to succeeding in your goals.

EXERCISE

# 4B

As all of us know, a critical element of any successful venture is to be very clear on what we are
attempting to achieve. In other words, it's important
to be aware of just what it is you are trying to do. In
terms of losing weight, this means being able to
"visualize" your *ideal body image.* While most
dieters can tell you vaguely how much weight they
would like to lose, very few have taken the time
to "picture" themselves exactly the way they would
like to be. This second visualization exercise ad-
dresses this issue. It is geared toward becoming
familiar with exactly how you would like to appear.
Simply saying that you would like to be "thinner,"
or "lose some weight," is not enough. You cannot
effectively begin to lose weight without some sort of
a plan. Use this opportunity to discover what your
real goal is. Once you have done so, you will be able
to implement your plan.

Begin every visualization exercise by following
the procedure outlined above. Close your eyes and
take several very deep, slow breaths. Let your body

and mind get into a very relaxed state, feeling very comfortable and peaceful.

Now picture yourself, in your mind's eye, as the person you see yourself to be right now. Imagine yourself standing in a familiar setting wearing familiar clothes (if you are wearing any). Now, with your eyes still closed, imagine yourself getting very large. Watch yourself grow, larger, larger, still larger. Imagine yourself even 100 pounds heavier than you are right now. See yourself as a balloon!

Now reverse the trend and watch yourself shrink. See yourself shrinking down well below your actual size. Watch as your body transforms from being very large, to being very small. Notice your reaction and mood swings. How do you feel? See if you can picture every detail of yourself, your head, shoulders, arms, torso, midsection, pelvis, legs, and feet. Notice everything shrinking down to miniature size. See yourself as thin as a pencil!

Now that you've noticed the two extremes, you are going to find your ideal body image. Imagine yourself transforming into the body you have always dreamed of. From the slimmest point you have pictured, imagine yourself growing into the perfect weight. Imagine your body parts filling out into your ideal shape and size. Remember that the ''perfect weight'' will permit optimal health. Don't go too far in either direction; you're searching for *your own* perfect body image. This is not the weight of anyone else, or the weight that society, advertisers, or Hollywood thinks you should be. Rather, it's the weight and size that *you want to be* and that *you are most comfortable with.* Let the picture vacillate between the highs and the lows until you have found the ideal and perfect point. Take your time, and enjoy the process!

Once you have found your ideal size and image, take note of what you look like. This is the weight that you are going to be. Remember that seeing yourself in your perfect image is the first, and most important, step toward achieving your goal. Notice as many details as you can. Picture your hips, waist, stomach, and legs. Notice the muscle tone, shape of the muscles, and their respective sizes. Remember that you can always change your vision and that you can return to your visualization anytime that you wish. Take just a moment to thank yourself once again for the person you are right now.

Change is wonderful, especially positive change, but a deep appreciation of yourself is among the greatest gifts one can receive. Know that you are okay just as you are right now, and that you are completely in charge of determining your own destiny. Once you are satisfied with your visualization you can open your eyes and smile!

Even though you are finished with this exercise, you can remember the picture as often as you like. Know that anytime you close your eyes, you can envision yourself as being your ''ideal weight.''

# 5

# Your Inner Guide

N ow that you are familiar with, and have practiced the skill of visualization, you are ready
to meet your "inner guide." This "inner guide," or
"advisor," as she is sometimes called, is available to
anyone and everyone who is willing to take the time
to meet her

Your inner guide is *not* a creation of "new age
thinking," nor is it a fancy term reserved only for
experienced meditators or visualizers. There is nothing artificial or superficial about it. In fact, as I
mentioned earlier, prominent surgeons and physicians such as Dr. Bernie Siegel, Dr. Martin Rossman,
and Dr. O. Carl Simonton are now teaching their
patients, and other physicians, the use and value of
such a friend. While many people approach this
subject with skepticism, a vast majority are very

glad they took the step. With increasing numbers of people now using their inner guides to help heal themselves of terminal diseases such as cancer, it seems reasonable to believe that we can benefit from some inner knowledge of what our bodies need to reduce or control our weight! In fact, we are far beyond mere speculation in this area of weight control. Increasing numbers of popular weight loss programs, such as "Sybervision" and other audio-cassette programs, are now incorporating elements of interaction with the subconscious mind into their programs.

Your inner advisor is inside your own mind. She is accessible and available only to you. Once you make contact with, and befriend, her, she will be with you whenever you wish. Your inner guide is a unique friend who can offer suggestions or guidance to any problem, concern, or question that you might have. Rather than being "stuck" in your usual way of viewing something, or narrow-minded, your inner advisor thinks spontaneously and creatively about every situation. She always knows what is best for you and can act as an invaluable companion for the rest of your life.

This special friend and source of guidance is sometimes referred to as your "intuition." Unfortunately, intuition has, to a large extent, been shunned and looked down upon in much of our culture. We have been taught to value, almost exclusively, our logical, rational, thinking mind. In doing so, we have learned to repress and even deny our ability to tune in to our intuition. Because society as a whole doesn't place a great deal of value on intuition, few of us have taken the time to connect with, or learn about this valuable source of insight. While many of us marvel at the wondrous ability that animals have to understand things seemingly beyond their mental capacity, we seldom, if ever, allow ourselves the same privilege. We conveniently refer to animals as having "instinct," but dismiss our own inner voice and intuitive nature as "meaningless" or "inconsequential." We do this while maintaining that we are the most "advanced" species that ever lived.

While an inner guide can appear in many ways, I advocate the method of connecting with some "special and wise person" in the mind. Because we are used to communicating with people, this makes the exercise easier to learn. In actuality, your inner guide can take the form of a plant, an animal, or virtually anything else that comes to your mind. The person (or thing) that appears may come as a vision, a sound, a voice, or some combination.

Contacting your inner guide is a procedure, similar in many ways to the exercises we have already learned in the previous chapter on visualization. Before we discuss the ways that your inner guide can be helpful to you, let's take a moment to meet her.

---

E X E R C I S E

# 5A

---

Close your eyes and take ten very deep, slow, and releasing breaths. With each exhalation, relax your belly, shoulders, and arms until all the tension has drained from your body. Check to be sure your legs and pelvis are relaxed and comfortable. As your breaths get deeper and slower, ask yourself, in a patient and loving manner, for a wise person to appear in your mind. Remember that a picture may or may not appear. Your guide can also appear in the form of a voice or a sound.

As you ask to be shown your inner guide, notice what types of images or voices begin to form in your mind. (Don't worry if nothing appears at first, or for that matter if nothing appears at all. You can always do the exercise again later, if necessary. One of the keys to any successful visualization exercise is to simply "let things happen" at their own pace.) As the images or sounds pass before your imagination's eyes (or ears), look at and listen to each of them carefully to see which one, if any, feels right to you. While it's true that there is no such thing as a wrong inner guide, there *is* one special guide who will be just right for you. With this in mind, take your time to make your choice. Do the exercise several times, if necessary, until you are very comfortable and happy with the one you have selected.

There is really only one guideline that should be followed to get the most out of this exercise. Unless the inner advisor is a representation of God to you, the guide you choose should be someone you *don't already know*. Your inner guide is someone you create, not someone you recreate. There is a very important reason for this. Very seldom, if ever, do any of us know people who are "all-knowing." This, however, is precisely what our inner guide is going to be to us. By using an inner guide who is a friend, family member, or someone we know, we are setting that person up as our "authority figure." In other words, we are giving away our greatest source of power to someone outside ourselves. Your inner guide is already a part of your unconscious mind. You are simply bringing to your consciousness what was previously unconscious.

Inner guides can last a lifetime, or they can change each time you call on them. I have found, however, that most people's guides stay with them for quite some time. As a person becomes comfortable with the guide, she seems to appear each time a situation calls for her.

At first it may seem to take several minutes to reach your inner guide. In time, however, all that will be necessary is the desire to make contact. All you'll have to do is close your eyes and call on her. As soon as you have contacted your inner advisor, you can immediately begin to communicate with her. For example, you can ask your inner guide a question that may be on your mind. Similarly, you can ask for a solution to a particular problem or concern you may have. Finally, you can ask for help or support during a time of crisis or need.

```
E X E R C I S E
5B
```

Assuming you have already met her, close your eyes and make contact with your inner advisor. Say hello to her (or him) and welcome her into your life. Thank her for being there for you. Remember that, by thanking her, you are actually thanking yourself, which is an important element of positive affirmation work. Earlier, we did a visualization exercise designed to determine your "ideal body image." Let's now use your inner guide to determine the "ideal weight" to go along with your new body image. Ask your inner advisor the question: "What is my perfect weight?" Then listen carefully to the answer you receive. Until now, you probably have been used to getting your answers primarily from your logical, rational mind. The answers you receive from your inner guide may be quite different from the ones you are used to, or they may be exactly the same. Trust in what you hear. It's coming from your highest and most accurate source of wisdom.

Now ask your inner guide a very important question: "What is it that I need to do to achieve this perfect weight?" Also ask: "How can I assure myself that I can achieve my goal, and how can I have fun doing it?" Trust that the answers will come, and that the ones you receive will be right for you. Remember that you are connecting with a higher, more intuitive part of yourself; thus the answers you receive may or may not be what you are accustomed to hearing. Likewise, the answers may or may not be logical at all. Give this technique a try and I believe you will be pleasantly surprised, not only in what you hear and see but also in your ability to incorporate the advice into your daily life. In this exercise, like all the others in this book, no one outside yourself is giving you commands or telling you what to do. You are asking yourself and getting answers from yourself, as to what the appropriate course of action will be.

DIFFERENT AREAS WHERE CONTACTING YOUR INNER
GUIDE CAN BE USEFUL:

**1.** *Ask your inner guide for answers or ways to work with specific questions.* For example, ask the question we mentioned above regarding your perfect weight. This and any other type of question can be answered quickly and easily.

**2.** *Use your inner guide to practice your affirmations.* Your inner guide is the wisest and deepest part of yourself. Thus, practice making contact with your inner guide, then asking her to repeat the affirmations you have been practicing. For example:

> Take a moment to close your eyes and relax. After taking several slow, deep breaths, see if you can make contact with your inner advisor. Once you have made contact, think of a positive affirmation you would like to share with your inner self. As an example, practice this one:
>
> I ONLY EAT FOOD THAT GIVES ME VITALITY AND LIFE FORCE.
>
> Now, have an imaginary conversation with your inner guide. Ask her to repeat after you the following words:

I ONLY EAT FOOD THAT GIVES ME VITALITY
AND LIFE FORCE.

Ask her to repeat the words three times, loud
and clear! Notice how you feel right now.
Notice how the words are reinforced, even
more, by having your inner guide repeat them.

3. *Speak to your inner guide when you feel you
   need support.* Whenever you feel frustrated
   or in need of support, your inner advisor is
   the perfect person to talk to. Any advice or
   encouragement you receive will be free of
   hidden agendas. The support you receive will
   come from knowledge and empathy, not
   from sympathy. Your inner guide will *always*
   listen to you and respond appropriately.

   Your inner guide can be a tremendous
   asset in your path toward a slimmer and
   healthier body. Be patient and trust that your
   inner knowledge will know what it is that
   you need. Don't be alarmed if answers do not
   come to you immediately, each and every
   time you make contact with your inner
   guide. There are times when your creative,
   intuitive nature is exhausted, just as there
   are times when your body is tired. If nothing
   happens, simply come back to the exercise
   at a later time.

   New opportunities are always presenting

themselves in which it is appropriate to connect with and/or consult with your inner guide. I encourage you to find unique and diverse ways to utilize this very special and effective friend.

Now that we have covered the preliminaries, let's move on to section two, which discusses the "overeating attitudes" themselves!

SECTION

TWO

·

# The
# Overeating
# Attitudes!

# 6

## I Always Eat When I'm Anxious

Certainly, one of the most common "overeating attitudes" of all is the complaint that "I always eat when I'm anxious." Most of us can think of instances (myself more than I'd like to admit) where we used food as a way to cover up an underlying sense of nervousness or anxiety about something in our lives.

Anxiety (or nervousness) runs rampant in our culture. Our hurried pace and complicated lifestyle are among the busiest in the world. In addition to the quick pace of our lives, each of us faces the daily issues of living in a society that places great importance on achievement, status, climbing the ladder of success, keeping up with others, and accumulation (the "more is better" syndrome). Perhaps an even more important source of our overall nervousness as a culture is the subtle way that anxiety itself is looked up to. We praise each other for being "too busy," and for having "excessive workloads." The most common excuse (and one that works well) for not keeping in touch with friends or loved ones is, "Sorry, I've been too busy to call." Some of us even brag (sometimes without even realizing it) about our husbands, our wives, our children, or ourselves for "taking on more than other people." Let's face it, despite being the most affluent country on earth and having tremendous advantages and blessings, the pressure to excel, achieve, and constantly be doing more places a great deal of internal pressure on each of us. This is true whether our primary emphasis is on raising a family, earning a living, taking care of ourselves or someone else, or any combination of the above.

Excessive busyness lends itself to anxiety. Anytime our lives are out of balance, or too busy, our internal homeostasis (equilibrium) is disturbed and is replaced with a feeling of uneasiness or stress, felt by us as "anxiety." Since both our physical organisms and our psychological makeups are totally unique, everyone will have a different tolerance for internal stress. This has nothing to do with being better or stronger than someone else. It simply means that some people can take on a greater amount of internal disharmony, or stress, than others before some action must be taken.

Stress, in and of itself, is not bad. It is merely a warning signal that there is a temporary disharmony within our bodies. Stress becomes a problem only when nothing productive and healthy is done to alleviate it. Stress, in the healthy sense, is actually a necessary and helpful indicator of how we are doing inside ourselves. It can be seen as an "internal watchdog" that maintains our inner health. Very simply, when we feel no stress, everything is probably okay. Conversely, when we feel anxious, something is wrong and needs to be changed.

We use food as a way to reduce a feeling of anxiety because it works! We've all felt times when, after eating too much, we became very tired. Food gives the appearance of reducing anxiety levels in much the same way. As our cells fill up with food, they temporarily lose their ability to feel anxiety. The more clogged our cells become, the less likely they are to be able to "feel." In this sense, food deadens our "internal watchdog." It puts it to sleep, thus taking away its ability to help us.

Food acts as a temporary diversion to our feelings of anxiety. Sometimes, when we feel anxious we can convince ourselves that we are hungry; other times we simply eat out of a reaction to our anxiety. Either way, food is *not* the answer we need. Even more important than the obvious problem of gaining weight, eating while we are nervous actually *in-*

*creases* the disharmony in our bodies. In other words, eating while we feel anxiety increases the level of stress in our body.

Healthy bodies can feel when their internal warning signals aren't working. Trouble can begin when there is stress in the body and the body's warning signals break down. Because its normal method of maintaining equilibrium has been disturbed, your body has to work harder to let you know that something is wrong. In working harder, the body creates even more stress, which takes a great deal of energy. In creating more stress, the body hopes to awaken you to the fact that something is going wrong. If you erroneously believe that eating food will reduce your anxiety, you are actually creating a war with your body. The more you eat to reduce your stress, the less you are able to feel the anxiety. This forces your body to create even more stress to let you know that something is wrong. The more you continue avoiding the *actual* source of your stress, the worse the problem becomes. Unfortunately, for many people, this vicious cycle can be broken only by some sort of physical breakdown. The internal stress, which started out as a simple warning signal, turns into an ulcer or even a life-threatening health problem.

The only reason we continue to use food as a diversion to our anxiety is because we don't feel that we have viable alternatives to replace it. The exercise for this chapter is designed to create an alternative.

It's the most important exercise in this book, in the sense that it's the basis for all the inner work that follows.

Meditation is a word that scares many people. Some of us associate it with going to India, the Far East, or other remote parts of the world. Others of us associate meditation with "sitting around," "being nonproductive," "entering realms reserved for yogis," or "taking years to master." While it's true that meditation developed in the East, many of our usual associations about its applications are incorrect. Today, millions of Americans utilize various types of meditation on a daily basis. In fact, our lifestyle lends itself to brief breaks in the day designed to bring harmony back into our lives. Meditation can be used to make us more relaxed, more peaceful, and yes, even more productive and effective! This latter benefit is what initially brought me (and millions of others) to meditation, and the former is what has kept me using it.

Meditation is not complicated, difficult to learn, or time consuming. In fact, it's one of the easiest things you will ever learn, and you will get more benefit from it per minute of practice time than from anything else you will ever do. In addition it's fun, it will take you only a few minutes a day, and most importantly, it can be used to eliminate most of the anxiety in your life! As you learn to deal more effectively with anxiety, you will lose the need to eat when feelings of nervousness arise. Remember, anxiety alone is not harmful. Only anxiety that is not effectively dealt with becomes dangerous.

Obviously this is not a book on meditation. I strongly encourage you, however, to read additional material on the subject to supplement what you will be practicing. I recommend Shakti Gawain's *Creative Visualization* and Larry LeShan's *How to Meditate* as valuable resources on this topic.

For our purposes here, we will be learning to relax our bodies and clear our minds. We will focus our attention in a way that will enable us to open to, and reduce the typical feelings of anxiety that occur for most of us throughout the day. The best way to learn to meditate is to practice, so let's begin!

EXERCISE

# 6A

Make a commitment to yourself that for the next ten minutes, you will allow yourself to take a mental vacation. No need to think of anything or solve any problems. Find a quiet, comfortable place where you can be all alone. Leave all your thoughts and problems outside the door.

All meditation is begun by relaxing the body as

much as possible. Loosen any restrictive clothing and get yourself into a very comfortable position. If you can sit in a chair or on the carpet with your back straight, it will prevent you from falling asleep, but this is not a prerequisite for success.

The breath is the tool that allows the body to relax. Close your eyes and take between ten and twenty very deep, very slow breaths. Pay close attention to the way your breath feels, and take your time. With each inhalation, picture in your mind a particular part of your body. With each exhalation, feel that part of your body completely relax. Breathing in . . . breathing out. Very deeply and very slowly. Feel your body enjoy the sensation of letting go.

Take a mental note of any area of your body that is not completely relaxed. Picture your breath going right into the constricted spot. You can tighten the area even more than it already is, and then simply let it go, allowing the tension to release from your body. Relax, release, breathe slowly, deeply, and easily, over and over again.

Anytime a thought enters your mind, simply acknowledge it, then let it go. Think of your thoughts as ripples in a stream. You can actually picture a stream in your mind if you wish. Thoughts will come up, but you don't need to give them any attention at all. Even problems, or sources of anxi-

> ety, such as things that need to get done, are simply thoughts to let drift downstream. Remember that for ten minutes nothing is important except your quiet time, your breath, and your relaxation.
>
> When you feel like you've had enough, very slowly begin to feel your body against the floor or chair. Slowly allow yourself to come back into your body. Bring your attention back into the room, and slowly open your eyes.

Notice how you feel. Notice how your level of anxiety has decreased by simply allowing yourself a few minutes to gain back some inner perspective and peace. Allowing the body and mind to relax, even for a few minutes, acknowledges to your "inner advisor" that she is doing her job. It lets her know that you felt her stress warning and that you chose to take a few minutes to "check in" with yourself. All that is required is a few minutes of quiet, focused time for yourself.

There is no "bad" time to practice an exercise such as this. Many people find that first thing in the morning is an excellent time, because the mind is usually less cluttered with typical worries of the day. I recommend that you practice this exercise for ten minutes in the morning, then for just a minute or two each time you feel yourself gathering any feelings of anxiety. This is particularly important if you feel yourself reaching for something to eat when you are nervous. Actually, practicing a short meditation such as this one is a wonderful thing to do before any meal. It helps clarify how much of your hunger is actual hunger and how much is merely anxiety. Practice this exercise as often as you can. It will get much easier and more effective with each practice session. Don't be shy about using the technique as many times per day as necessary. It will help to reduce your level of anxiety, thus enabling you to avoid eating out of nervousness.

# 7

I Always Eat When
I'm Bored

⬩

If I had to guess, I'd say that eating when one is bored is the most common overeating attitude of all. I've hardly met a person who, at some time or another, hasn't eaten as a response to boredom! Like all overeating attitudes, eating out of boredom is simply a habit that can be dealt with, given the right mind-set and belief system.

Boredom stems from the belief that where we are is not good enough: that if only we were doing something differently, doing more, or spending our time in another way, things would somehow be better. All of us have experienced boredom at one time or another. Boredom is a feeling of emptiness, a lack of excitement, a feeling of wanting something to happen.

We eat when we are bored in order to pass time: to divert our attention from our feelings of emptiness. Eating provides us with a feeling of instant gratification, a temporary relief from our inner suffering. Eating is something to do, a way to keep us from having to look honestly at our feelings. Just as we saw was true in chapter 6 on anxiety, eating numbs our awareness of how badly we really feel.

The problem with using food as a solution to *any* uncomfortable feeling, including boredom, is that the relief we feel is only temporary. The moment we stop eating, the feeling returns. In this sense, eating isn't a solution but rather a diversion.

Unlike some overeating attitudes, such as eating out of anger, eating out of boredom is relatively easy to detect in ourselves. This may be due to the fact that eating out of boredom is a "socially acceptable" thing to do. Advertisements encourage it and friends support it. "Got nothing better to do, let's go out and eat!" is the message. I recently saw a television advertisement promoting a popular beer. The essence of the message was: "Rainy nights are boring unless you drink our alcoholic beverage." Of course this is completely absurd but nonetheless it's somewhat consistent with our beliefs as a culture! It's often looked at as "unthinkable" to spend time with someone without including either eating or drinking in the plans.

Like all overeating attitudes, eating out of boredom originates in the mind. Our minds control our attitudes, our feelings, and consequently, our behavior. Thus, it is only through learning to control our minds that we can free ourselves from destructive habits.

In a certain respect, eating out of boredom is an ironic problem to have developed in our culture. This is because one of the most common complaints of the day is the problem of "not having enough time to do the things I would like." Instead of gravitating toward all the things we wish we had time for, when we feel bored we have developed the habit of reaching for food as something to do. As mentioned above, food is viewed as a form of instant gratification. It's a mindless activity that requires no effort. We don't need to work or even think about what we are doing. In this sense, it's easier to reach for food than to search for healthier alternatives.

"Awareness" is the first, and most important, step toward conquering this overeating attitude. Being aware of our use of food as a diversion from our feelings of boredom is paramount to creating a successful solution. Once awareness of the problem is established, the rest is relatively simple. What remains is finding useful inner exercises to substitute for our tendency to eat.

The first exercise for this chapter is designed to help break the pattern of reaching for food when you experience the feeling of boredom. It gives you something to do in those first few moments when you are used to going for food. As always, these initial moments of an uncomfortable feeling are critical to overcoming a problem that is habitual in nature. It's those first few moments when the temptation to reach for food is usually the greatest. Again, this is usually due to lack of acceptable alternatives. Exercise 7A is a quick form of meditation, which provides the needed alternative.

The second exercise for this chapter challenges the notion that food is something that necessarily must be included in our social communication with others. Going out to, or having people over for, breakfast, lunch, dinner, dessert, a drink, ice cream, or the like, is only one way—not the only way—to enjoy the company of others. The pattern of eating with family and friends is a long-standing tradition that is not necessarily the best use of our intimate time together. While almost no one subscribes to this philosophy, you will at least hear another perspective.

> # EXERCISE
> # 7A

What are the things you would like to do if you really
had the time? Would you read more books, learn a
foreign language, or take up a musical instrument?
How about devoting a few minutes a day to meditation or yoga? What about catching up with old
friends, returning or making phone calls, writing
letters, or writing a book? How about learning
to make new things, sewing, working in the yard,
getting more organized, or cleaning out closets?
This list could go on for pages! The point is that all
people have things they have always wanted to do
but couldn't find the time to do. It might be something you'd love to do, or it might just be something
that would make your life easier if you did it.

Take out a piece of paper and begin your list.
Feel free to borrow some of the suggestions on my
list above, or totally discard them and come up with
your own. Think of as many items for your list as
you can.

This exercise is about "association." You are
simply going to begin to mentally associate any

feelings of boredom with "doing what I always wished I had time for."

Take some time to look over your list, and keep a copy with you, or at least close by, for the next few weeks. You'll want to refer to it often. Whenever a feeling of boredom begins to surface with you, close your eyes and practice the following brief meditation:

As with any form of meditation, begin the process by taking several deep, slow breaths. Feel your body relax with each passing exhalation. Deeply breathe in the clean, fresh air, and breathe out any remaining tension and stress.

As your body relaxes, make contact with your inner advisor, whom you met back in chapter 5. Welcome her into your heart and invite her to share some wisdom with you for the next minute or so. Remember that your inner advisor is nothing more than a deeper, wiser part of yourself that is capable of adding perspective and knowledge to any question or concern you may have.

With a relaxed body and mind, and while continuing your breathing, ask your inner advisor which activity on your list you wish to do at this time. Tell her that you are aware that a feeling of boredom is nothing more than an opportunity to spend some time doing an activity that until now you didn't have the time for. You may want to run through your list in your mind, or even open your eyes gently and read through your list slowly. (If you choose this option, simply close your eyes when you're finished reading and focus your attention back on your breathing.)

Your inner voice will tell you which of the activities you should focus your attention on at this time. It may come as a sudden insight or a subtle feeling. The way it comes is different for everyone. Don't worry if it takes a few minutes. The answer will come in its own time.

If you get in the habit of doing this exercise whenever you feel bored, you will be amazed how many new activities will enter your life. You might also be surprised at how efficient you become at doing things you are truly interested in. For example, it takes only a few minutes a day over a period of time to learn a foreign language, become relatively proficient in meditation, or even to learn a musical instrument. If you commit to practicing this exercise instead of eating when feelings of boredom surface, you could be on your way to a new skill in no time. Give it a chance. I think you'll enjoy it!

## EXERCISE
# 7B

This exercise is important because it demonstrates how much emphasis we put on food out of pure habit, rather than out of hunger. It also demonstrates how dependent we have become on food to supplement our time with others. This is tremendously important for the subject of this chapter because dependence on food as a social partner reinforces our pattern of eating out of boredom.

The idea is to begin to change the pattern we have established of always eating (or drinking) when we spend time with family or friends. I know that sometimes it's both necessary and preferable to do so. I'm not suggesting that we change *every* future social engagement we have. Rather, the idea here is to begin to question whether food needs to be a part of our social get-togethers.

Begin by calling up two or three people you enjoy spending time with. Schedule some time to just simply be together. No meeting at a restaurant, or planning a meal or coffee together. Just good old-fashioned communication.

I was surprised how difficult it was for me to break my own pattern in this area. Calling friends just to get together seemed somehow empty or incomplete. After getting used to the idea, however, I soon realized that my communication with the person I was spending time with was actually more enjoyable than before. Instead of dividing my attention between my friends and food, my friends were given my undivided attention. Breaking my habit of bagels and cream cheese twice a week has also saved me thousands of calories per month that served more of a social role than a function of curtailing hunger.

This exercise will help enormously in breaking the habit of reaching for food out of boredom. It reinforces the idea that food was meant as a source of nourishment, not entertainment! It will take only a few meetings with friends for you to discover that you can appreciate your time together even more than you used to. In addition, you will begin to appreciate what you do eat because you will be doing so out of choice, not habit.

# 8

# I Always Eat When I'm Angry

◆

**M**ost of us have eaten as a response to feelings of anger at one time or another. Unfortunately, for many of us, this is more than a "once in a while" occurrence. Like so many other habits in our lives, eating as a reaction to anger can become a pattern that is difficult to break.

Anger is nothing more than a learned reaction to frustration. It comes about when we feel that something or someone is acting inconsistently with the way we would prefer it to be. When faced with circumstances that are not going the way we would like them to, we tell ourselves, in one way or another, that things "shouldn't be that way." We then select one of a number of familiar angry responses to rid ourselves of the feeling. Eating is one of the most frequently chosen of these responses.

There's no question that we live in a society that reinforces the belief that "anger is bad." There seems to be a sort of unspoken feeling that anger should be held inside, dealt with privately and quietly. The problem with this philosophy is that it fails to address reality. The fact is that people sometimes do get angry. The relevant point isn't whether or not people actually get angry, but rather how they choose to deal with, and express, their anger. The belief that anger is somehow bad, in and of itself, breeds what is called in psychology "passive aggressive behavior." This is where a person, in an attempt to avoid showing his feelings of anger, finds what he believes to be socially acceptable alternatives to express that anger. These alternatives stem from anger but don't appear to be aggressive. This occurs, for the most part, without any awareness on the part of the individual expressing the anger. It is an extremely common phenomenon, and you can guess what one of the most frequent expressions of "passive aggressive behavior" might be. Right: eating!

Eating is a method that many people have learned to use as an acceptable way to vent their anger. This is a difficult area to relate to, as a reader, because if you are utilizing this strategy, you are probably doing so unconsciously. In other words, you aren't saying to yourself, "Gee, I'm really mad right now. I think I'll vent my feelings by eating a lot of food." Instead, reaching for food is most likely an unconscious pattern you developed out of an attempt to "not feel" the anger. Your unconscious goal becomes reaching for food before you have the time to feel the extent of your anger. This unconscious strategy protects you from the possibility of expressing your anger in other ways that are considered unacceptable by yourself and by society.

Using food as an expression of "passive aggressive behavior" is a subject that I'm personally very familiar with. I used the unconscious technique for many years before I finally realized what I was doing. I got into the habit of reaching for food whenever I was confronted with something that made me angry, particularly if it was something I didn't think *should* make me feel angry. It was an interesting period of time for me because most people, including myself, thought of me as someone who "didn't get mad very much." It wasn't until later, when I took an honest look at myself, that I discovered that I was actually angry more than I would have liked to admit.

To create substitute alternatives for dealing with anger, we need only to find effective methods that not only prevent us from eating as a reaction to anger but also allow us to deal with our feelings of anger more honestly. By all means give vent to your anger I'm not an advocate of repressing emotions. Rather, I'm suggesting that there are alternative. more effective, and healthier ways to deal with feelings of anger other than by eating, which only serves to cover up the feelings.

The first, and most important, step toward finding these viable alternatives is the recognition that we have at least the tendency toward this overeating attitude. Because of the denial aspect of passive aggressive behavior, this can be a tremendously difficult pattern to detect. Seeing your own process in action requires a *true* commitment toward introspection. Allow yourself to be very honest in your assessment of how you handle your anger. While you may *not* have this tendency, you would certainly be in the minority. You may need to think back over the past few times you got "really mad" at someone or something. What did you do shortly thereafter? Did you go to the kitchen, or out to a meal to "vent" your feelings? Think carefully and see if you can detect a connection between angry feelings and reaching for food.

After recognizing a tendency to eat as a response to anger, the next step is to create substitute responses that, in effect, replace the eating. Unlike other overeating reactions, such as anxiety or tiredness, which become more likely over time, eating as a response to anger often occurs within minutes, or even seconds, after the feelings of anger arise. This is because the feelings of anger are greatest the moment they are first felt. Thus, in order to be effective, our solutions are ones that need to be immediately available to us. The following two exercises can be practiced whenever a feeling of anger arises in your mind. They are extremely effective and healthy alternatives to eating as a response to anger.

EXERCISE

# 8A     Time Warp

This exercise is appropriately called "Time Warp." The idea is to temporarily postpone your anger by creating an imaginary period of time between your feelings of anger and the way you choose to express them. This is a very effective and legitimate form of alleviating frustration and anger and is frequently taught by hypnotherapists and psychologists alike.

Unlike many other emotions, anger doesn't allow us the luxury of finding a quiet and comfortable location to implement an exercise. To the contrary, anger is an emotion that requires an almost immediate solution. "Time Warp" is an ideal technique to deal with anger because it can be called upon effectively in a matter of seconds.

The technique itself goes something like this: When a feeling of anger arises in your mind, close

your eyes and take a very deep breath. With practice, this can become an almost immediate response. Regardless of how intense your feeling of
anger happens to be, imagine that the circumstances that created your feelings of anger happened
last week, not ten seconds ago! Irrespective of how
silly or unrealistic this might seem, it really works.
For example, let's suppose your two-year-old spills
a glass of milk on the carpet five minutes before
your boss and her husband are scheduled to come
over for dinner. Under normal circumstances, it
would be easy to see how a situation such as this
could elicit a temporary feeling of anger or frustration. This is not true, however, if the same thing
happened last week. It's often easy to maintain a
philosophical outlook about things that are over and
done with; it's not always so easy to do so at the
time they occur. What "Time Warp" does is allow
you to experience the situation as if it occurred in
the past, therefore creating a sense of distance
between the actual event and your reaction to it.

This exercise can be used in almost any situation where you find yourself feeling angry. Again,
the relevant part of the exercise is to imagine that
the event, whatever it was, happened sometime
in the past.

If we eat as a reaction to our feelings of anger,
then we must create ways to soften our feelings of

anger, at least long enough to gain some perspective. Again, most eating due to anger happens very rapidly after the feeling of anger is first felt. In other words, we reach for food as a way to express and/or reduce our feelings of anger. This being the case, "Time Warp" is a potentially effective solution. It provides an almost instantaneous relief from the feeling of anger, allowing you to choose not to eat as a reaction to the frustration.

EXERCISE

# 8B

## The Flame Meditation

As was true with Exercise 8A, this exercise is designed to be used the moment a feeling of anger is felt. It allows you to feel the anger while at the same time creating a psychological distance between the feelings of anger and any harmful reactions (eating) to those feelings.

Begin this exercise by closing your eyes and getting yourself in a comfortable position. Take several deep breaths, and allow yourself to relax.

Begin breathing in fresh air, and as you do,

imagine the breaths themselves being rays of white light. Each inhalation is an individual stream of pure and peaceful white light. Breathe in, breathe out . . . breathe in, breathe out.

As you exhale, feel your body relax. Let all the old air escape from your body. New air comes in, old air goes out.

With your eyes still closed, picture a burning fire in front of you. The flame can be any size you wish, from a single candle to a roaring bonfire. See it clearly before your eyes. See not only the flames but also the size of the fire, and its distance from you.

Think of something that makes you angry. It can be anything you wish. There's no such thing as "wrong" when it comes to anger. Picture the situation, event, circumstance, whatever it is, before your eyes. Feel the feelings of anger that you associate with this situation. A key to this exercise is to allow yourself to really "feel" the feelings.

Now breathe in the white light and breathe out the anger into the flames—breathe in the light and out the anger. Over and over again. With each exhalation, picture the angry feelings being smothered by the flames, which are then replaced by the soothing white light that comes in the next inhalation. Breathe in more fresh air, then out with the anger. Continue with this process until all feelings of anger have been felt, and then released into the flames.

Feelings of anger don't have any special appearance to them. They can look like whatever you wish. Some people picture them as black air, others as creepy monsters. Whatever you associate with anger is right for you. Simply feel the anger, breathe in white light, then release the angry feelings, whatever they look like, into the flames.

This exercise can be effective at a moment's notice, irrespective of what causes the anger. The instant you feel angry you can breathe in white light and breathe out the feelings of anger. This exercise, like the one before it, creates space between the feelings of anger and the likelihood of eating as a response to those feelings.

# 9

## I Always Eat When I'm Tired

◆

Eating when we are tired is a very common thing to do. Somewhere along the line, probably very early on, we learned that food was our primary source of energy. While it's true that food provides the necessary nutrients to sustain life, it's a nutritional misunderstanding to believe that food is a solution to everyday tiredness or a viable source of immediate energy.

Tiredness can be caused by many factors. One cause of tiredness is simply physical or mental fatigue. Human beings need a certain amount of rest to stay alive, healthy, and alert. Many experts believe that eight hours of sleep per twenty-four-hour period is more than sufficient for the average person. But what about the other causes of tiredness? Why, if we get even close to eight hours of sleep, do we walk around feeling so tired so much of the time? Certainly stress and physical exhaustion can play important roles. Even more important, I believe, is the choice of what and how much food we eat. Think of your last Thanksgiving dinner as an example of overeating. Imagine what it felt like to eat well in excess of what you actually needed. Recall the feelings of fullness, lack of mental clarity, and tiredness that resulted from too much food.

Every time we overeat, we are in a sense having another "Thanksgiving dinner." Our bodies, however, can't differentiate between holidays and any other day of the year. What our bodies do experience is simply whether or not there is enough food to nourish them, or whether there is too much to digest. Whenever there is too much food inside our bodies, our digestive systems are forced to work overtime to complete their function. This extra work takes a tremendous amount of physical energy and leaves us feeling exhausted. This is true irrespective of how much sleep we are getting.

There are two ends of the eating spectrum. On one end there is chronic overeating, the Thanksgiving dinner we were talking about, that leaves us feeling stuffed and uncomfortable. On the other end there is "fasting," a complete refraining from eating altogether for some undefined period of time. We all know what we feel like after a huge meal. We tend to feel tired, run-down, and lethargic. Those of us who have fasted know that the lack of congestion in the digestive tract can actually create a tremendous feeling of energy, a natural high of sorts. While I'm not advocating fasting as a specific practice for anyone, I do feel it's important to point out the comparison that many people may be unfamiliar with. The point is that food is *not* necessarily a legitimate way to eliminate the tiredness that occurs after a long day's work or play. In fact, food can actually make us even more tired than we were before we ate it. It's important, then, to distinguish between being tired and actually being hungry. Once we understand that food will not take away our tiredness, it then becomes critical to discover *when* we are eating as an unconscious attempt to rid ourselves of fatigue. This is not to say that one can't be hungry and tired at the same time, which of course is entirely possible. Rather, the goal is to clearly distinguish between actual hunger and physical or mental tiredness.

"Being tired" can often bring back unconscious childhood memories of being fed. When we were upset and crying as youngsters, our parents had only a few guesses as to what might be wrong. For the most part, we either needed to be changed or held, we weren't feeling well, or we were tired or hungry. Chances are that at least some of the time our parents guessed wrong. In other words, there were many times when we were simply tired and needed to sleep but instead, we were given a bottle or some-thing else to eat. Certainly this was a harmless error, and no one was to blame. There was no way to tell exactly what we needed 100 percent of the time. It's interesting, however, to begin to think of the mental associations we made as children about tiredness and food. If, at the same time as being fed, we were also held lovingly in our mothers' arms, it would have been unusual *not* to have associated being tired with also looking forward to food. Obviously, we can no longer cuddle in our mothers' arms, as we once could, but we can still "reach for the bottle." I don't think the exact psychological implications are tre-mendously important here, but it's hard to deny that there is something comforting about food after a long, hard day. The important point is to begin to recognize that there is an association between being tired and reaching for something to eat.

The problem of "always eating when I'm tired" stems, in part, from what is called the "reactive mind." This is a part of the mind, within the sub-conscious, that acts as a linking system between the normal human feelings that come up for all of us and the way that we respond to those feelings. There are many feelings that are affected by this "linking system," but some of the more common ones in-clude tiredness, anxiety, boredom, anger, and frus-tration.

I think of the reactive mind as a sort of "trigger system" that initiates destructive behavior when any of these (and other) feelings come to mind. Of course the destructive behavior I'm referring to in this book is eating at times *other* than when we are actually hungry. The way our "trigger system" operates is quite interesting. First, we experience a feeling that is in some way uncomfortable. Since this chapter focuses on tiredness, we'll use this as our example. At some point in our lives, we came to believe that eating would supply us with needed energy. Assuming we would rather feel energized than tired, our "reactive mind" associates ridding ourselves of the undesired feeling (tiredness) by searching for something to eat. Because this process was unconscious, we quite naturally began to associate tiredness with being hungry, until at some point the association became automatic. Consequently, when we get tired, the *tendency* is for us to feel hungry. The process works in very much the same manner for feelings of irritation, anger, boredom, or anxiety. Each of us will have our own reactive associations between certain feelings and food. Which specific associations we have is dependent on which feelings make us uncomfortable. Our own individual psychology and upbringing will determine which themes are predominant.

If you assume, as I'm suggesting, that there are instances where we eat as a reaction to certain feelings we experience, then the trick is to find effective ways to control our "trigger systems." If we can learn to avoid eating as a reaction to tiredness, for example, we will eliminate one of our major sources of overeating. Eventually, the idea is to become completely conscious about what, and how much, we eat at all times. With practice, we will become so in tune with what our bodies are hungry for that we will catch our trigger systems before we act on them.

By this point you're already familiar with the usefulness of skills such as meditation and visualization. It will probably come as no surprise, then, that the most effective method to monitor our trigger system is a form of meditation. I have designed an exercise that I find extremely effective, first in helping to distinguish between real feelings of hunger and simple tiredness. Once this has been established, you can make a more conscious decision about whether or not you desire food.

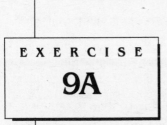

EXERCISE

9A

This exercise can be done before walking into your kitchen, or anywhere else you intend to eat, if you feel tired or if you have recently finished working/ playing for an extended period of time.

For this exercise, it's best if you allow yourself

to lie down in a comfortable position. Close your eyes and take ten very deep breaths. Allow your body to relax and unwind. Feel the tension drain from your muscles as you continue your breathing.

Make a connection with your inner guide or advisor. Say hello and welcome her into your inner conversation. See if she has anything special to say to you. As you continue to breathe, ask your inner guide to help you answer a question. Tell her that you would like some help in deciding what it is your body is in need of, if anything, in the way of food. Let your guide know that your original intent was to get something to eat. You're checking with her, however, before your final decision, because you know that sometimes all of us associate feeling tired with feeling hungry.

Ask her, "If I could go to sleep right now, would I? Would my body appreciate a nap, an extended period of sleep, or even a few minutes of quiet time? How does my body feel right now? Am I tired? Am I hungry? Am I sure? If I am hungry, would I remain so if I rested for ten more minutes?"

Give your inner self plenty of time to respond to your questions. Take some time to tune in to how you really feel. Allow your relaxed feeling to continue. Notice how, as your body takes this short time out for rest and clarity, it begins to feel more rested, and less hungry.

As you ask yourself these questions in a very relaxed state of mind, you are far more likely to get an accurate response than if you simply allow your reactive mind to take over. Perhaps your inner self gave you the message that what you really wanted was some rest. Perhaps you discovered that you truly were hungry. Either way, you are the winner. You are not trying to deny yourself food, but rather you are attempting to find out your real feelings. By taking the time to "check in" with yourself, you are eliminating your "trigger response" toward food. Many times you will find that you are indeed hungry. Very often, however, you will discover that all you needed was some time to unwind.

The beauty of an exercise such as this is that you are creating more options for yourself. Whereas before you may have reached for food as a "trigger response" to a feeling of tiredness, you can now reach for food, *or* you can take a few minutes to see if you still really want it. Again, it may turn out that you are hungry, but why not find out for sure?

# 10

# Exercise Is Boring

Millions of people don't exercise at all. While people report many reasons for their lack of activity, one theme stands out as the predominant excuse in this day and age where most people understand the value of exercise. I can hardly remember a day where I haven't heard the statement that is the title of this chapter, "Exercise is boring."

Contrary to popular opinion, the belief that exercise is boring was not "inherited" or even learned from our parents. Rather, it is a simple lack of creativity derived from a perception we have about what exercise actually is. It is my belief that if you think that exercise is not enjoyable, you simply haven't found the ideal combination of physical activities.

I have two firm beliefs about exercise. First,

regular physical activity is a major key to a firm, trim, and happy body. Secondly, there is a perfect form of exercise for everyone. Looked at together, these two statements suggest that anyone who is physically able is capable of achieving lifelong physical fitness.

Why is exercise considered an "overeating attitude"? Very simply because the belief that exercise is boring is one of the most destructive beliefs that we can have in regard to our weight and our level of physical fitness. This is true for two major reasons. First, every other attitude discussed in this book is somewhat individual in nature. In other words, each of the other attitudes can be looked at, and worked with, alone. So it's possible to master one attitude, and still be working on another. For example, we can learn to avoid eating because we are anxious, but still be practicing techniques to avoid eating as a reaction to tiredness. Unfortunately, this can't happen with exercise. If you don't exercise, you don't exercise! The second reason this particular attitude is so destructive is because you can't afford the luxury of believing that exercise is boring; it's simply too important. Exercise is the second half to the weight loss equation. While getting a handle on overeating is obviously paramount to weight loss, developing a healthy approach to physical activity is an equally important element. Exercise is like tightening the bolts after putting together a piece of machinery. While you can't tighten the bolts prematurely, you certainly wouldn't want to avoid the process all together. You need both to complete the job.

Exercise is an almost magical ingredient to any weight loss program. In addition to the obvious advantage of burning calories and fat, exercise contains several additional characteristics worthy of mention. First, physical activity actually reduces appetite. I frequently feel hungry before going out for my morning run, only to return without the least trace of hunger. Secondly, exercise helps us work with each of the other overeating attitudes. For example, it is now widely accepted knowledge that exercise greatly reduces anxiety and stress. If you always eat when you're anxious, and you find additional ways to reduce your anxiety, you are, by definition, going to eat less as a result. In addition, people who love to exercise are almost never bored. I have a list a page long of physical activities I love to do when I am fortunate enough to have the time. Consequently, I never eat simply because I'm bored. The list goes on and on! Exercise is helpful in combatting virtually any overeating attitude you can think of.

If we assume that most people would like to enjoy exercise *if they could,* the important question becomes, "How do we learn to enjoy something we thought we didn't like?" My approach to lack of activity is quite different from the views of most "authorities" on physical fitness. Unlike many people, I don't believe people should force themselves to do anything related to exercise. Forcing yourself to jog three times a week is merely reinforcing an already strong preference against exercise. Going to the gym may be fun for some people, but is a complete drag for others. Swimming can be a peaceful experience for many people and a form of purgatory for others. A different, and far more effective, way of looking at your distaste for exercise is to assume that you need to be more creative in your selection of activities. I have yet to meet a person who, after closer examination, couldn't find at least one activity that qualifies as a legitimate and enjoyable form of exercise that the person also enjoyed doing.

Everyone who feels that exercise is boring has a different reason underlying this belief. For many, the feeling of "not having enough time," seems to be at the root of the problem. "My life is very busy, and I can't do everything" is a very common complaint. For many people, time is their most valuable asset. Unless something is very exciting or time efficient, they simply won't squeeze it into their already busy schedule. Coming to this conclusion can be a tremendous asset in creating an eventual solution. I have a friend who is a business executive in the San Francisco Bay area who serves as an excellent example. He was a self-proclaimed, "all-time opponent to exercise." He felt that exercise was not only "boring," but even more importantly, he discovered that he believed exercise was "a terrible misuse of his valuable time." This insight into the reason behind his belief about exercise was critical to his ultimate solution. For him, everything was boring when compared to business! The only way to come up with an effective solution, then, was to find a way *not* to disturb his business activities. When my friend put on his "creativity hat," he came up with an exercise program that, given his preferences, is among the most creative I have ever seen. Most of his time is spent meeting with people on a variety of business subjects. Since he was unwilling to alter his daily scheduled meetings, he had to come up with a solution that incorporated exercise into his normal day. He decided that one of his daily meetings would be a "walking meeting." Now, every day, he takes a one-hour walk with another person. When people call to schedule time with him, his secretary informs them of his policy. If someone wants to meet with him, they either put on their tennis shoes and join him for his walk, or they have to wait until another day. Now, instead of being stuck inside an office building all day long, his days are broken up with a brisk walk out in the fresh air. Twenty pounds later, he feels better than ever. He has found that he enjoys his "walking meetings" more than he ever could have imagined.

If a serious and productive business meeting can turn into a full hour of fun and healthy exercise, I'm convinced that most other activities can be altered in much the same way. This is true regardless of the *reason* you think exercise is boring. Maybe you never had fun exercising as a child, maybe you were ridiculed for not being the best athlete, or perhaps your family didn't value exercise while you were growing up. Whatever the reason, expanding your perception of what exercise is all about is the key to finding an enjoyable form of physical activity. Exercise is not limited to the types of activities we usually think of. Running, hiking, skiing, playing tennis, and swimming are only the tip of the iceberg when it comes to legitimate forms of exercise.

The exercises for this chapter are designed to help broaden the way you view exercise. Pull out a piece of paper and prepare to be very creative.

EXERCISE

# 10A

This first exercise involves writing down every conceivable form of exercise you can think of. Begin with popular types of exercise such as running and swimming, and move outward toward less traditional forms such as horseback riding and climbing rocks. The important point here is to begin to get

a sense of the enormous variation and number
of different types of exercise. Much more effective
than simply reading a list of available exercises is
sitting down and thinking of them yourself. Think of
as many as you can, and if your mind goes blank,
think of the dozens of different sports represented in
the summer and winter Olympic Games.

After you have compiled your first list, take a
few minutes to look over what you have written. Pay
particular attention to the exercises that look the
most appealing to you. Regardless of the "practical-
ity" of undertaking a certain exercise, focus on the
ones that look like the most fun. For example,
kayaking might be an exercise that looks like a lot of
fun but seems unrealistic due to the nature of the
sport. Forget about realism! If something sounds
like fun, put a check mark beside it. Try to pick out
at least three forms of exercise that sound appealing
to you.

The next part of the process involves a visualization exercise. If you need to, refer to chapter 4 on
Visualization for the precise procedure to this skill.
The key to this particular visualization exercise is to
"see" yourself participating in the three forms of
exercise that you picked from your list. Imagine
yourself not only participating in the activities but
also preparing for them. This might include traveling
to and from the activity, as well as purchasing or

picking out any required gear. The idea here is to see yourself participating in the sport or physical activity that seems the most fun to you. There is no reason you can't allow yourself to spend some time exercising in the way that you choose. Remember that the first step to accomplishing a goal is to "see" yourself, in your mind's eye, achieving whatever it is you are attempting to do. If you've never allowed yourself to choose a physical form of exercise that's fun, it's due, at least in part, to not "seeing" yourself in the activity.

E X E R C I S E

# 10B

The second exercise for this chapter is geared toward discovering ways to incorporate physical activity into your daily life. Although this is not meant to be a substitute for a regular exercise program, it can be a useful way to exercise your body with little or no inconvenience or alteration to your normal daily schedule. (Remember my friend's clever walking meeting.)

Begin by making a list of a typical day's activities. Include aspects of your work, chores, child care, errands, etc. Anything that you do almost every day should be included. For example, you might take the kids or the dog outside to get some fresh air or for a short walk every day. Perhaps you take the bus or the car downtown to work or to the store. Maybe you take an elevator to the eleventh floor twice a day, five days per week. Everyone has a routine of some kind. The idea here is to get some of it down on paper where you can take a look at your options.

The next step is to begin discovering ways to turn a routine that you have to do into some kind of physical exercise. Most of the time, turning a routine activity into a viable form of exercise involves little more than increasing the frequency or duration of that specific activity. For example, if you choose the example above of bringing the kids, or the dog, out for a short walk, you would simply need to increase the time spent in that activity. More often than not, a greater amount of time is spent in the preparation phase of an activity than in the actual activity itself. This means dressing the kids, finding the leash, locking the door, etc. Since you're already spending the time in this "preparatory" period, why not increase the time and effort in the part of the activity that you originally set out to do?

Increasing a five-minute walk to a twenty-minute
walk takes fifteen additional minutes. Those fifteen
minutes, however, probably represent only a frac-
tion of the actual time you need to spend in the
overall activity. Again, you have to get yourself out
the door anyway—why not make the best of it? In
this way, you can add almost two hours per week to
your exercise schedule without any additional
"wasted time." What this really amounts to is
maximizing the efficiency of certain activities that
are inherently related to exercise. It's nothing more
than getting creative! If you add just a little speed to
your walk, your twenty minutes a day can turn into a
really great workout!

The same principle applies to going up an
elevator or even getting to and from work. Remember, it takes time to wait for the elevator just as it
does to walk. Many times, I've walked up steps and
arrived quicker than someone I was with who
chose to ride the elevator. The same is true with
parking your car. It often takes ten or fifteen minutes to find a "good" parking spot. What's so great
about wasting fifteen minutes of your time looking
for a "close in" spot when you could be spending
that valuable time walking? Even people who park in
parking lots can sometimes change their choice of
parking lots to ones that are slightly farther away.
What's so magical about a close in location? Try

parking a half mile from work every day. You'll get great exercise, you'll spend hardly any additional time, you'll probably be thinking more clearly when you arrive, and you'll have time to "unwind" when you leave. You can take almost any daily routine and turn it into a form of exercise. Be creative!

# 11

## I Always Eat Out of Habit

◆

**M**any of us were habitualized from early childhood to eating dinner (and our other meals) at essentially the same time every day. This habit suggests that, rather than eating out of a conscious decision based on hunger, we were trained to eat according to the clock. As the years went by, we became so accustomed to eating at regular intervals that we actually begin to feel hungry based upon the time of day. Have you ever heard yourself or someone else say, "Oh my gosh, it's seven o'clock and I haven't eaten yet. I'm really hungry," or something similar? Boy, I sure have!

There was a time in our lives when eating at

regular intervals was important, if not essential, to our health and our growth. Babies need almost constant nourishment to keep up their strength. Those of us who are parents recognize that "first thing in the morning" is an important, and often convenient, time to feed our children. Other times of the day become our regular eating times as well. We tend to give children a snack sometime in the mid-morning, followed by lunch around noon, an afternoon snack, and a regular dinner time.

For most of us these "regular eating times" were probably the times we received the most positive attention from our parents. Everyone at the table was telling us how good we were and how cute we looked. People were busy feeding us, loving us, and telling us how wonderful we were. In a sense, we were in heaven and what a wonderful life it was! Most of our waking day was spent centered around food in one way or another. It seemed that all we had to do, to be appreciated, praised, and loved, was to continue eating. No amount was ever "too much." This being the case, what motivation did we have to change our habits? None!

Is it any wonder that we continue to place so much attention on food in our lives? Hardly. The fact is, that much of our most influential and molding years were spent thinking about little else. In terms of learning to control our weight today, it's important to recognize how these patterns began and see them for what they are. These patterns of relating to food are mere "carryovers" from our childhood. We learned how much importance to place on food by the actions and behavior of our parents and family. We can see, however, upon close examination, that no one is to blame for the development of these patterns. At the time, the emphasis and concern for food was a necessary and important part of our development. It was offered out of love.

Over the years our eating patterns developed into rituals, or habits, which were reinforced by society. The result was that, rather than altering our eating habits to match our developing and changing needs, we maintained our existing patterns.

There are many examples of how our family, and society, reinforced our eating habits. Here are just a few that illustrate the point. I'm sure you'll begin to see many others as you read through the list.

1) *Whenever we cried or appeared to be unhappy, an easy solution was to give us something to eat.* Whoever was giving us the food would rationalize this behavior by saying, "Oh, she's just hungry." This was probably the easiest way of getting us to be quiet. This isn't to say that sometimes we weren't "just hungry," but rather that every time we were upset it wasn't the only possible explanation. Think about the hidden message we received each time we cried and then were fed out of habit rather than need. We learned that whenever we were upset, or didn't feel quite right, the best solution was to get

something to eat. Do you, or does someone you know, ever eat when not feeling on top of the world emotionally?

2) *Every night we ate dinner at the same time.* Eating dinner at the same time every night presupposes that every night you are hungry at the same time. This, of course, isn't true and thus doesn't make much sense as a realistic way of eating. There *were*, at one time, many reasons why eating dinner as a family at the same time every night was a good idea. This was a time for everyone to come together and share. It was also, perhaps, the only time when all members of the family were in the same place at the same time. It was an opportunity to be together as a family. It was comforting and fun to share experiences at this very special time. In addition to being a "special time," it was certainly more practical for everyone to eat together. Obviously a family of five eating at five different times would create numerous problems—dishes, cooking, and a big mess, not to mention lack of important family communication and sharing.

It is not my intent to criticize family dinners. I still enjoy sharing a meal with each member of my family, as well as the family as a whole. My intent is only to demonstrate how we developed the eating patterns we still have today and why food is such a major issue in so many of our lives. You can see how we learned to associate food with good times, family communication, attention, and love. At the time, the act of eating was an experience that far exceeded anything else (in terms of personal satisfaction) that we did during the day.

3) *Advertisements.* The influence of advertisements on our lives is enormous. Everywhere we look or listen, whether it be television, radio, newspapers, magazines, or billboards, advertisements are attempting to convince us to eat something for any number of reasons—*except for hunger.* Advertisements try to get us to eat or drink something because it's "sexy," or because someone else will love us more because we eat it. They also try to get us to eat something because "everyone else is eating it," or because it's the "in" thing to do. They will use whatever means are necessary to get us to eat something, whether or not we're hungry. Advertisers are very aware of the hidden reasons people eat food. They know that people eat to get themselves to "feel better," or "to gain someone else's approval." They also know that people eat out of habit rather than out of hunger, that people associate eating with having fun with friends and family, and that people associate food with feeling loved. With all this knowledge about the reasons people eat, it's easy to see how advertisements can affect us on many different levels of awareness.

Each of these three examples (and there are many others) demonstrates how we learned and receive reinforcement daily about the importance of "eating out of habit" rather than out of hunger. We can see that patterns such as eating continuously throughout the day, or eating dinner at the same time daily (whether or not we are hungry), came about for a reason. When we were small children, it was *necessary* to eat throughout the day, beginning first thing in the morning. Eating with the family was also a positive thing to do as it gave us time to be with each other and to share a common experience. There is also nothing inherently wrong with looking at, or watching advertisements, so long as you are aware of what they are attempting to do.

When *any* activity becomes a habitual response, it needs to be looked at as a possible destructive force in your life. The fact that you've always eaten dinner at six P.M. isn't reason enough to continue doing so. If you think it is, you are acting "unconsciously," rather than consciously, regarding your decisions about food. In terms of losing weight, becoming "conscious" about our eating habits is a primary step for success. Becoming aware of your "habitual" patterns is the only way you can move beyond them.

In what ways do we regularly act habitually in our eating habits? Any time we eat simply because it's "dinner time" (or breakfast time, or lunch time, or noontime, or snack time, or whatever), we are exhibiting habitual qualities. Similarly, any time we eat to "avoid being hungry later," we are acting habitually. Until "later" arrives, it's impossible to tell whether or not we'll be hungry at all.

Our habitual characteristics do not stop with eating. We also become habitualized into giving ourselves unconscious negative messages about eating. We give ourselves dozens of negative messages every day that are entirely unconscious in nature. Here are a few examples of the types of messages we give ourselves every day without even thinking about them: "Everyone in my family has a weight problem." "Every time I eat dessert I gain weight." "I hate to exercise." "Diets are hard." "I'll never lose weight." "My family has big bones." "I inherited my weight problem." "It's in my genes." The list goes on and on! We can all think of many messages we give ourselves without ever stopping to think about the consequences. These words have become such a habit in our lives that we seldom think about what we are really saying. Each time we repeat one of these types of statements, we are giving ourselves the message: "I CAN'T LOSE WEIGHT." Each negative statement is registered in our subconscious minds as *absolute truth.* The more often we repeat these types of statements, the more habitualized they become until at some point we *don't even realize we are saying them*! Start listening to people around you. See if you can pick up how many negative, self-defeating messages the average person gives himself or herself on a daily basis. I think you'll be astounded. Even the bumper stickers, posters, and T-shirts reminding us of our inadequacies in ways that are supposed to be funny are almost always giving us negative messages, which only serve to remind us how incapable we are as human beings, and how difficult it is to lose weight. T-shirts that say "Born to be fat" may seem funny to some, but I assure you they won't help you in your efforts to lose weight. They are reinforcing a cruel message that will encourage your subconscious mind to believe that you are incapable of positive change.

One of our goals is to be consciously aware, at all times, of the messages we are giving ourselves. If we are not, we will simply end up replacing our old habitual messages with new habitual ones. Even though positive messages of any kind (habitual or not) are infinitely more productive than negative ones, they are nonetheless less effective than they might otherwise be. For example, suppose you are repeating the affirmation, **"I eat slowly and enjoy my food,"** but you are doing so out of habit and because you think you "should be," instead of consciously, with thoughtfulness and care. The effectiveness of the message will be greatly reduced because you haven't put your full attention on the words you are saying. You are repeating the words without meaning, without really being aware of what you are affirming. While you want to allow positive affirmations to become a regular part of your life, avoid letting them become a mere habit that is practiced unconsciously.

Concentrate on every affirmation and exercise you are learning in a conscious, heartfelt way. Practice less often if you need to, but offer your full attention when you do. As you consciously replace your old beliefs with new ones, you will be putting an end to the part of yourself that is "habitual." You will be opening yourself up to the fully functioning human being you are capable of becoming.

EXERCISE

# 11A

## Inventory of Habitual Beliefs

This exercise is geared toward becoming more fully aware of the types of messages you give to yourself on a regular basis. Just what do you think of yourself? As is true with most other exercises, it's best to practice this one in a quiet place where you can be alone for a period of time. Allow yourself to become very relaxed and calm prior to beginning. A calm mind always thinks more clearly than an agitated one. Take a few very deep breaths before you begin.

Think about all of the labels, messages, and ways that you think of yourself. Anything having to do with food, diets, weight, exercise, etc., is fair game for this exercise whether positive or negative. What is "truth" for you? Do you think of yourself as thin, fat, lazy, energetic, unable or unwilling to exercise? Do you think you have a large appetite? These are only a small handful of potential questions you can ask yourself. What you're really looking for here are the beliefs you have about yourself that you think of as "indisputable," or as "just the way I am."

Many of our beliefs about ourselves are so "fixated" that we are hardly aware they exist. We simply accept them as a part of us that is destined to be there always. Spend plenty of time thinking about and writing down each of your beliefs. It's only after you become aware of the beliefs that you have about yourself that you can begin to work on changing them.

This exercise enables you to begin to see the ways that you trap yourself by your own labels. How can a person who "loathes exercise" make a legitimate effort at finding activities that will burn fat from her body? Very simply, a person who loathes exercise will continue to resist beginning an exercise program, *but* making the "inventory list," may enable her to discover things about herself that she might not be aware of. For example, she might discover that she does, in fact, dislike exercise but that she loves walking the dog. She may never have associated walking the dog as a "legitimate" form of exercise. After writing down her beliefs about herself, however, she may find ways to enjoy exercise even though she doesn't like exercise.

A second important point to this exercise is that, after writing down their beliefs about themselves, many people discover that they have been pretty hard on themselves. They start to ask themselves important questions, such as: "Why don't

I like exercise? Was it because I didn't get praised
for it when I was younger? Was it because I had
a few bad experiences with physical activity when I
was a child? Was I ridiculed for poor performance
twenty-five years ago? Are these good reasons to
deny myself the privilege of enjoying exercise?"

Exercise is only one area that you'll be able to
look at with a completed "inventory." All aspects of
weight control are equally applicable. The important
point is that inventories have the potential to "stir
up" our consciousness and give us the opportunity
to look at, and think about, beliefs that may or
may not be appropriate to keep.

# 12

## I Have a Big Appetite

◆

Have you ever stopped to ask yourself why it is your appetite is the size it is? Chances are you haven't. The fact is that your appetite is *exactly* as big as you think it is. The belief "I have a big appetite" is one of the most common overeating attitudes around. Fortunately, however, it's one of the easiest attitudes to work with.

Belief systems are very powerful because they determine how we see the world. If we believe strongly enough that we have an "enormous appetite," then how in the world will we ever stop overeating? The only way this will happen is by changing the beliefs we have about our eating. Think for a moment about what would happen to your appetite if you **absolutely believed that, without question,** you "eat like a mouse." We've all heard people make statements like that about the size of their appetite. How could a person who was sure she "eats like a mouse," overeat? She couldn't possibly do it very often because she believes so strongly that she "doesn't eat very much."

I'd like to suggest that the people who grow up believing that they have small appetites were not the fortunate few who were born with them. Rather, over time, they developed the personal belief system that they had small appetites. Through a combination of the mental and verbal messages they gave themselves, and the way they visualized themselves in their minds, they developed the belief that they had small appetites. The key, then, to those of us who believe that we have "big appetites," is not necessarily in changing our diets as much as it is in first changing our attitudes and beliefs about our appetites. Our level of food intake will adjust to what our beliefs about ourselves allow.

Many of us grew up hearing statements like: "What a good boy you are; you have such a big appetite," or "Mary's a good girl because she always eats all her dinner." In addition, many of us heard guilt statements, such as, "You'd better eat everything on your plate because there are millions of starving people in the world." These statements and guilt techniques are some of the ways that our parents tried to tell us that they loved us. They are also a large part of the reason that we developed the belief that we were born with a large appetite. When we understand the reasons we develop a belief system it becomes much easier to implement a change. In addition, once we realize that other people helped to convince us of the size of our appetite, we can then decide to make our *own* decisions about how much we choose to eat and how we feel about it as a result. We can decide that we are "good" people, without eating everything on our plate or demonstrating that we have a large appetite. In fact, we can decide that we are good people without eating anything at all. Similarly, if we feel bad about the starvation in the world (which is a very real problem), we no longer need to feel powerless or guilty about the situation. In fact, we **can** do something about it! We can donate our time, energy, or money to one of the hundreds of valuable service organizations dedicated to feeding the hungry all over the world. The fact is, however, that overeating is hurting, rather than helping the problem. Rather than overeating out of a sense of guilt, why not try taking the difference between what you eat *after* reading this book, and the amount you used to eat, and donate it to your favorite charitable food drive?

Just how good about yourself do you feel today simply because you can eat everything on your plate? Does your self-esteem flourish because you have a "good appetite"? Of course not! Needless to say, you are not the person you were when you were one or two years old. Why, then, do you tend to carry on the same old eating patterns? The answer is that your subconscious mind developed a belief system that was validated by repetition. Each time you heard the words, "You're a good person because you ate everything on your plate," you gained a sense of gratification that led to a temporary feeling of increased self-esteem. You felt better about yourself because you learned that all you had to do was to eat a lot of food to be praised and loved. Since all of us want to feel better about ourselves, you naturally "took the bait," or in this instance "took the food," as a means of instant and easy gratification. What could possibly be easier? As you grew older, you stopped hearing the praise from others, but your subconscious mind went right on believing the same old message. It kept believing, or at least hoping, that more food would result in that feeling of self-esteem. Your subconscious mind has never been retrained to believe any differently: Hence, the result is that you believe that "having a big appetite" and "eating everything on your plate" will reward you with a boost of self-esteem. Your subconscious mind literally thinks that you *want* a big appetite!

Belief systems develop by the words we hear from others and by the messages we give to ourselves as a result. Since we cannot change the words we hear from others, the solution is to begin changing our belief systems and attitudes about our appetites by changing the words we give to ourselves. The first step in eliminating the destructive beliefs we have about our appetites is to change our internal messages from negative to positive. We need to reprogram our subconscious minds to include the real and truthful facts of today, which include the actual size of the appetite we want.

The following affirmations are meant to address the issues of the size of our appetite and whether or not we really need to eat everything on our plates. With practice, they will help us begin to change our belief systems about our appetites.

---

## MY APPETITE IS SMALL: I ONLY EAT WHEN I'M HUNGRY

---

Now repeat the statement again three times as if you really mean it! Say it with conviction. Remember you are changing belief patterns that developed when you were only a child.

---

## MY APPETITE IS SMALL: I ONLY EAT WHEN I'M HUNGRY

◆

## MY APPETITE IS SMALL: I ONLY EAT WHEN I'M HUNGRY

◆

## MY APPETITE IS SMALL: I ONLY EAT WHEN I'M HUNGRY

---

You should practice this affirmation often, but particularly five minutes before sitting down to eat. Keep reminding your subconscious mind that you only need to eat small amounts of food to feel satisfied; your appetite is now small and you feel satisfied as a result.

Sometimes a "large appetite" is caused by a subconscious fear that we're going to be hungry later. We subconsciously feel that by eating large amounts now we can avoid what we believe will be an uncomfortable feeling later on. The result, however, as we all know, is exactly the opposite. As we overeat, we actually become hungry again in a shorter period of time. As was true with the development of the "size of our appetite," this fear about lack of food may have developed when we were very young. We may have been punished for not eating everything on our plates by our frustrated parents who felt it was important for us to keep up our strength. I've heard many stories from people who were forced to sit in their high chair for literally hours, prohibited from moving until they finished every last morsel. In addition to sitting for hours in front of our plates, we may have been threatened that we would "never eat again" unless we finished our meal. As parents ourselves, many of us may have tried these techniques on our own children. We know how effective they can be at getting a child to comply. Imagine being confronted with a soggy plate of cauliflower and at the same time wondering whether or not you would be able to eat tomorrow. I am not making a value judgment on what types of parents we are as a result of attempting to get our children to eat. What I *am* doing is demonstrating the reason we develop our fears and beliefs about food in the first place. By being forced to eat everything on our plates, we quite naturally developed a fear, if not a phobia, about not having enough food. Being praised for being a "good eater" only added to the problem and again reinforced how important it was to eat. When we stop to consider these very powerful messages we received as youngsters, it's hardly a wonder that "normal diets" usually don't work. In order to lose weight, and particularly to keep weight off, we *first* need to erase the subconscious fears we have that we're going to be without food. Otherwise, we will feel compelled to revert to old patterns, which feel comfortable and safe.

Again, the best way to change a fear is to change the messages we give to our subconscious minds. The second affirmation for this chapter helps us change our beliefs about the importance of eating everything on our plates and also eliminates the unconscious fear of being punished as a result.

---

## I CAN ALWAYS EAT LATER IF I'M STILL HUNGRY

---

This is a very powerful message, which can be practiced both before and while you eat. Since you are eliminating fears and concerns that developed very early in your childhood, you may not even be aware of the fear at all. With that in mind, repeat the message again three times with meaning, determination, and conviction.

I CAN ALWAYS EAT LATER IF I'M STILL HUNGRY

◆

I CAN ALWAYS EAT LATER IF I'M STILL HUNGRY

◆

I CAN ALWAYS EAT LATER IF I'M STILL HUNGRY

Enjoy yourself as you practice the affirmations in this chapter designed to help free you from your past. As you determine the actual size of your appetite, and drop your fears about "not having enough," you will find that overeating is something you simply don't need to do.

# EXERCISE
## 12A

Pull out a piece of paper and prepare to draw two pictures of yourself. Don't worry if you feel you aren't an artist, for no one has to see your work. It's only for you. The drawings can be as simple or elaborate as you wish. Personally, I draw simple pictures, similar to stick drawings.

For the first picture, make a drawing of yourself exactly as you see yourself to be. Again, don't worry about the quality of your drawing, but do pay particular attention to the proportions of your different body parts. For example, if you feel your legs are longer in comparison to your torso, express it in your picture. If you feel you have wide hips, or a slender face, do the same.

Now draw a second picture of yourself, only this time draw the figure as you feel you would really like to be. Take your time and think about exactly what it is you would like to achieve in terms of changing your body. Don't exaggerate, but rather be as specific as you are able.

After completing both drawings, put them side by side and analyze the two. Look very carefully at the first, then the second, and finally make the comparison. Look closely at the drawing of how you would like to appear. Notice each feature of your body and how it would change from the way it is now. Look again at the first drawing and then back to the second. Imagine what it would take to transform from one to the other.

This exercise is based on the assumption that it's very important to be extremely clear about one's goals. Many people who spend a great deal of their lives wishing to lose weight haven't stopped to think about *exactly* what it is they are trying to accomplish. Everyone can say, "I'd like to lose twenty pounds," or "I'd like to fit into a size 6," but many times this isn't specific enough to accomplish the goal. The problem is that it's very difficult to achieve an important goal without first knowing *exactly* what the goal is. In fact, the more important the goal, the more important it is to clarify the parameters. Imagine trying to get to a specific place on a map but having only a vague idea where it's located. Weight loss works very similarly. Although all of us know that we'd like to lose some weight, just wanting it isn't usually enough. We need to be clearer about what our goal actually is.

Many psychologists have found that self-drawings are a very powerful way to diagnose, as well as to express feelings. Drawings, because they

are visually oriented, tend to impress upon the
subconscious mind the message you are trying to
convey. Therefore, if you take the time to draw a
picture of how you would like to appear, and compare it to a picture of how you perceive yourself
to be, your subconscious mind can relate to what
you are attempting to do. It allows your subconscious mind to say, "Oh, I see. This is where you
want to be." This is an excellent exercise to practice
once a week, because both your self-perception and
your goals may change frequently as you lose
weight. Each time you do this exercise, you will be
reinforcing to yourself the direction you wish to
take. You will find that, as you become more and
more clear on the exact dimensions of your goal,
your appetite will begin to adjust accordingly. Your
subconscious mind will begin to make the connection between a smaller appetite and your desired
result.

# More "Food for Thought"

# 13

# Self-Criticism

♦

**H**ow would you feel if you saw your parents for the first time in almost a year and the first thing that one of them said to you was: "Gee, I thought you were on a diet—what's wrong?" If you are like most people it wouldn't do much for your immediate sense of self-esteem. Criticism is another major "overeating attitude" that needs to be addressed. For our purposes, we're particularly interested in "self-criticism." If hearing criticism from others is painful, unhelpful, and unnecessary, why do we spend so much time and energy focusing our attention and our spoken words on our own shortcomings, faults, and problems?

Most people live their lives in what is called a "deficiency model." This means that virtually all of their attention is placed on their personal shortcomings. When thinking of themselves, deficiency-oriented individuals usually focus on the ways they can improve or get better. These people are very self-critical, judgmental, and angry toward themselves. There is always an enormous gap between where they are and where they would like to be. They look in the mirror, they see fat; when they talk to others, they say such things as "I need to lose five pounds." When they lose five pounds, they always discover that, lo and behold, it would be even better to lose five more! Their whole lives are filled with thoughts and actions designed to make them "better." The deficiency model of living is absolutely insatiable. A person living life in this manner can *never* be happy or satisfied because as one deficiency is cleared up, another one immediately replaces it.

"Well, of course I want to get better and improve myself. Don't you?" This is how a person living in the deficiency model would react to any questions about his attitude and way of living. Most people with this mind-set don't see any alternatives to their habit of consistently berating themselves with criticism. They feel that, if they want to lose weight, they'd better be real hard on themselves and focus on what's wrong. After all, isn't that the only way to succeed?

We are fortunate because there *is* another way of communicating with ourselves. I refer to this more positive alternative as the "growth model." The growth model says: "Of course I can get better,

I can always improve, **BUT, I'm also okay just the way I am.**" The difference, while it might seem small, is nonetheless very significant. The growth model is very accommodating to attitudinal work on ourselves. It reminds our subconscious minds that we are very capable people who deserve to be treated with love. The deficiency model, on the other hand, serves as a constant reminder to our subconscious minds that we are "not good enough" and are incapable of change. As we have seen, this is the very belief system that interferes with successful weight loss.

Constant criticism, like all negative reinforcement, is only a poor habit. It's very destructive and rarely changes anything. When you tell someone, especially someone you love, how they ought to change, or be different, the most frequent reaction is for them to pull away from and disregard your comments. People don't really want or need us to tell them how they should be, unless, of course, they ask us, which is quite a different situation. If people want to change, they will do so in their own time and in their own way. While most of us can see how this type of pattern works with others, we very seldom see it in ourselves. We tend to forget that we, like others, need *positive* feedback in order to feel good about ourselves; without it, it's virtually impossible to cultivate the needed self-esteem to succeed at weight loss. It doesn't do any good, in terms of results, to tell ourselves over and over again how fat we are, how poorly we're doing, and how much weight we have to lose.

The growth model is not a prescription for denying ourselves the ability to change. On the contrary, it's the very attitude that *encourages* positive transformation. Criticism, as an overeating attitude, serves as a constant reminder to our subconscious minds that we are incapable of achieving a desired result. Remember that the subconscious mind registers everything we say, positive or negative, and then tries to validate it. When we are critical of ourselves, constructively or otherwise, it's simply more reinforcement of the negative attitudes toward ourselves which helped to create our weight problem to begin with.

When we work from the growth model we are paving the way for positive changes in our lives. As we expect to lose weight, and remind ourselves how capable we really are, we are allowing our subconscious minds to facilitate growth. As our minds open to our potential, our bodies can follow suit by losing weight. Criticism is inconsistent with these goals and needs to be eliminated as a means of communicating with ourselves.

The more comfortable we become with giving ourselves praise and recognition, the more we will be able to see the wasted energy that is expended in criticism. The point is not that we can't or shouldn't improve ourselves, but rather that the only *effective* means to improvement is through a changed attitude that includes self-love and positive affirmations. Smothering ourselves with a constant list of our personal shortcomings will not, in *any way*, help us to achieve our goals. It will only serve to reinforce, once again, the very messages we are trying to replace. Through positive affirmations we can replace our need to criticize with a genuine feeling of gratitude and love for ourselves. It is through this positive feeling toward ourselves that we can succeed in our goals.

## ◆ How Success Comes About

A related concept to the uselessness of criticism is the idea that **success always comes from what we can do,** and never comes about from what we can't do! While this may seem obvious, most of us do not live our lives under this precept. To the contrary, most of us spend a great deal of time worrying and complaining about things over which we have no control.

Anything that is *over*, whether it occurred ten years or just ten minutes ago, cannot be changed. Anything that cannot be changed is not worthy of our attention and focus. For example, the fact that you've "always been overweight" has no bearing on or relevance to what can be done about your situation. Reminding yourself or talking about the fact that you've always had a weight problem won't do anything to solve the problem.

Similarly, if you "blew it" last night by eating too much dinner, it's too late to not have done so. What you CAN do is learn from the past and decide *not* to eat too much **tonight;** you CAN remind yourself how much better you feel when you **eat correctly;** you CAN decide to start up a new exercise program, and you *CAN* practice your affirmations, visualizations, mental exercises, and inner work.

Think about your own patterns and attitudinal habits for a minute. Think about all the energy you expend thinking about things that cannot be changed, events that are over and done with. Promise yourself that, from now on, you will avoid focusing your attention on situations that are beyond your control. Likewise, promise to avoid giving yourself the types of negative messages that reinforce the very things you are attempting to change. Instead of expending valuable energy on things that cannot be changed, choose to focus your efforts on areas that can be of help. This is the very essence of attitudinal work.

E X E R C I S E

# 13A

The next time you're at a cocktail or dinner party, listen carefully to all the criticism around you. Listen to the way people criticize others and themselves. After going home, take a few minutes to reflect on all that was said. Review the criticism and somehow tally it all up in your mind. Now sit back in your chair and decide for yourself exactly how much good any of it did in terms of achieving a desired result. You may decide, after thinking about it, that when you get right down to it the criticism does no good, it contributes virtually nothing to any desired result. You'll probably decide that success comes from deciding what it is you *can do* to improve yourself, not from reminding yourself about past failures. See if you can apply this conclusion to your attempts to lose weight. Focus on what you can do, instead of on how poorly you're doing. Wherever you are in your weight loss process, this attitude will facilitate the greatest amount of success. I guarantee it!

# 14

The Value of
Positive
Expectations

•

Jesus said, "When ye pray, believe ye have it."
One interpretation of his message might be,
"Work on the assumption that what you want, you
already have." This is one of the greatest keys to
successful, life-changing inner work. You must believe in your heart that what you want, you not only
*can* have but in a sense already have. Imagine a child
on Christmas Eve. He pictures in his mind the wonderful new little toy he is going to receive. When he
awakens, he smiles in wonderment at what he sees
before him. He doesn't waste time or energy thinking about all the reasons why he won't get the toy.

We attract into our lives those things and events that we think about the most, are most certain about, believe at the deepest and most internal levels, and imagine and rehearse in our minds the most vividly. Have you ever found yourself mentally rehearsing an "uncomfortable situation" prior to the actual event? Remember how every detail of the situation became very clear in your mind? Think about how many times an uncomfortable event created in your mind actually became reality. The same can often be said about other areas of our lives. Tiredness and our health are a few of the many examples. Have you ever gone to bed after looking at the clock and noticing that it was way past your bedtime? If so, you may have awakened in the morning expecting to be tired. After all, you only got four hours of sleep! The question becomes, was it really the fact that you had only four hours of sleep that made you so tired, or was it the overwhelming expectation that you were going to be exhausted? Have you ever heard ads on TV suggesting that it's "flu season"? Maybe you expect to catch colds in the winter. If you do, you can bet that you get sick more often than someone who expects to remain healthy. The fact is that when we *expect* negative or fearful experiences in our lives, our expectation of those events attracts those very experiences! On the other hand, if you are used to expecting positive experiences in your life, and in your mind you envision satisfaction, happiness, and success, you are much more likely to experience these types of situations than if you do not.

Issues with our weight work in much the same manner. Most of us who perceive ourselves to be "overweight" have expectations about ourselves that severely limit our weight-loss efforts. For example, if we *expect* to eat too much, we probably will. Similarly, if we expect to be bored while jogging, it will probably happen. Every expectation we have about ourselves, positive or negative, greatly increases the likelihood that our experiences will match those expectations.

The mind loves expectations of any kind, because they give it something to strive towards. Expectations do not, however, have to be created by our past experiences. Just because you ate too much at the last party does not mean you will do so again at the next. Just because jogging around the block was boring last year does not mean that jogging in the park has to be boring today. One of the most limiting, and I believe unfortunate, of all human tendencies, is to believe that our future has to be dictated by our past. It simply isn't true. I can think of dozens of personal examples where I made a conscious decision to expect something to have a positive outcome and it was followed by a positive result. For example, I used to have a tendency to overeat at cocktail parties. I always expected to reach for too much food because I perceived myself to have no willpower. Just for fun, I did a visualization exercise where I imagined myself at an upcoming party. I visualized the beautiful trays of food displayed around the room and saw myself walking right past them without any desire to reach for them. By mentally rehearsing the event prior to actually being there, I was creating an expectation for myself not to overdo it. Consequently, since that time, I have learned to "expect" willpower from myself. I no longer arrive at a party thinking, "Oh no. Here I go again." Rather, I have confidence in myself based on my self-created expectations.

Affirmations are another area where expectation levels play a major role. For example, let's assume you are practicing the affirmation, "**I only eat healthy food that nourishes my body.**" If you believe in what you are saying and *expect* positive results, the message will have far greater meaning to your subconscious mind. If you visualize yourself eating healthy food, see yourself enjoying it, and expect positive results from yourself, your chances of success will go up exponentially!

Unlike the child who pictures success and rewards in his mind, we as adults often spend sleepless nights wondering why we are *not* succeeding. We ponder our weight the way we sometimes ponder our finances, relationships, and other sometimes worrisome areas of our lives. Rather than focusing on what's going "wrong" in our lives, our attitudes and thoughts must be changed to focus on what's right—on what we are doing to improve our situation. In a sense, it's safe to say that all worry about weight is a complete waste of energy and is only counterproductive. This is because it takes our attention *off* our positive expectations about our weight and puts it back on our old belief system that said, "I'm not doing well enough."

Individuals with positive expectations about themselves are "results-oriented" people. This is the opposite of people who have negative expectations about themselves, who are "problem-oriented." One of the major differences between successful weight loss and unsuccessful weight loss lies in the expectations we place on ourselves. Problem-oriented people will tell themselves over and over again how terribly they are doing and will keep expecting themselves to fail. They will very seldom disappoint themselves because they are so sure about the direction they are headed. They have set up a belief system about themselves that prohibits, rather than encourages, success. If we believe we are incapable of change and destined for failure, there is no way our bodies can respond other than by remaining in a "weight gain" pattern. Fortunately, the reverse is equally true. If we believe, as results-oriented people do, that we are bound to be successful, then we are very likely to find a way to succeed. We know that all we have to do is find the optimal way to achieve our goals. Our minds and bodies will automatically look for ways to validate the fact that we are losing weight. We are insisting that there is a way to succeed, rather than looking for a way to fail.

Inner work is ultimately nothing more than a series of instructions to ourselves. These instructions are the *only* way our bodies know how we want them to respond. Thus, once we begin giving ourselves positive instructions, our bodies will begin the process of responding.

Our bodies intuitively know that they are always on either a "vicious" or on a "virtuous cycle." A vicious cycle is one in which the body is hearing negative messages from the subconscious mind about how poorly it is doing. The body then responds by keeping itself in a "weight gain" cycle by feeding itself with the wrong kinds and the wrong amounts of food. The body believes, based on the instructions it is receiving, that we want it to perform poorly. A virtuous cycle, on the other hand, is one where the body is receiving positive and loving instructions from the subconscious mind. In a virtuous cycle, the body responds by feeding itself only when it's hungry and then only with nutritious food. We are always giving our bodies instructions of one kind or another. It's up to us to make the decision of which types of messages we want it to receive.

The power of expectation cannot be underestimated. Already in your life, you can think of numerous examples where you had positive expectations about your potential that preceded a positive outcome. You may have advanced in your job, passed a course, learned to run a mile, or played a great game of tennis. Whatever the example, you *first* must have believed that you could do it. You could see yourself succeeding *now*. Some people may respond to this statement by saying, "Sure, but that example doesn't count because it was easy." The reason something is easy is because you can see yourself succeeding first! Controlling our weight works in exactly the same way. As soon as we are **sure** we are going to lose weight, so it is. Many people think, "Well if only I could first prove to myself that I could lose the weight, *then* I'd be able to expect to keep it off." This is understandable because it's the attitude most of us have been taught since early childhood. Nevertheless, this attitude is one that needs to be changed. Instead of "believing it when you see it," start, "seeing it when you believe it." This means that you must *first* decide that you are a thin, fit, and healthy person; then, and only then, will you allow yourself to become one. It's not the other way around, as most of us have come to believe. We can begin the process by visualizing ourselves as the people we would like to be. We can start telling ourselves, and seeing ourselves, as thin and healthy people. At that point, we will become such people. As long as we tell ourselves, "I know it's difficult for me to lose weight," it has to continue to be a difficult and boring job for us because we haven't yet begun to see ourselves as succeeding. Our expectation of difficulty will dictate our ability to succeed. The process is similar to learning how to run a mile. The minute we start to believe in ourselves, to believe that we do have the capacity to do it, we are on our way to success!

There are a few affirmations for this chapter that practice the idea of positive self-expectation. Slowly repeat to yourself the following words:

---

### I AM ALREADY THIN

---

Now close your eyes and repeat the same words slowly to yourself, this time at least three times. Visualize yourself as fit, trim, and healthy. Remember to put love and meaning into the words. You must *believe* the words as you say them. Feel the power of the words as you repeat them to yourself.

---

### I AM ALREADY THIN

◆

### I AM ALREADY THIN

◆

### I AM ALREADY THIN

---

It's time to put an end to *all* self-defeating expectations you have about yourself. From this moment on, promise yourself that you will never again discuss the reasons why you can't lose weight, or for that matter why you can't do anything else. All negative expectations are barriers to self-improvement. By giving yourself positive, thin, and loving suggestions, you are setting the stage for rapid and continual weight loss. The first step in all successful weight loss, or in any goal in your life, is to start telling yourself that you are absolutely capable of success. You must believe yourself to be capable of achieving whatever it is you are striving to accomplish.

With this information in mind, please practice the following affirmation:

---

## I LOVE MY BODY, AND I FEED IT CORRECTLY

---

Again, remember the importance of meaning and commitment to your words. Try it again with your eyes closed. Your body is a gift from God. It carries you and goes with you wherever you go. You have a lot to be thankful for. This time, repeat the affirmation three times with **love, commitment,** and **meaning.** Again, remember that the most important element of success is to see yourself as *ALREADY THERE.*

I LOVE MY BODY, AND I FEED IT CORRECTLY

✦

I LOVE MY BODY, AND I FEED IT CORRECTLY

✦

I LOVE MY BODY, AND I FEED IT CORRECTLY

After you repeat the message to yourself, stop for a minute and notice how you feel. Notice the way your body softens as a result of the loving message you have just given it. Think for a moment about what you have just said to your body. You have told it, with loving kindness, that it *matters* to you.

## EXERCISE
# 14A

### A Truly Positive Expectation!

The exercise for this chapter is a lot of fun! The next time you go clothes shopping I'd like you to buy yourself the outfit of your choice, with one major difference from the way you usually do it. Rather than buying an outfit that fits you, buy the size that you want to be. Don't think about a single reason why you shouldn't do it. Expectations are intuitive, not logical. After you buy the outfit, spend a small amount of time each day visualizing yourself wearing it. This may be the first time you have ever exercised total faith in your ability. Good for you! By doing so, you will be sending another positive message to your subconscious mind, which says, ''I am certain that I am able to lose any amount of weight that I choose. I have positive expectations about my abilities.'' Have faith in yourself and in the positive expectation that you are going to lose the weight.

# 15

# Reprogramming

◆

Our minds are filled with thoughts and beliefs that dictate our behavior. The more ingrained these thoughts and beliefs are, the more difficult they are to change. The concept of reprogramming simply means taking out of our subconscious minds those thoughts and beliefs that are destructive, harmful, and counterproductive and replacing them with new beliefs that are positive, result-producing, and hopeful. In this sense, every exercise in this book is a form of reprogramming!

Our minds are like sophisticated computer systems. Computers, however, while quite sophisticated, are not as complicated as many of us think. When you get right down to it, they really do only one thing: they follow specific instructions. Computers will always, 100 percent of the time, do exactly what you tell them to do, and nothing else. If you feed them useful and accurate information that is exactly what you will get from them. If you make mistakes in your programming or in entering information, mistakes will *always* show up in the results. Like computers, our minds are programmed *only* to follow instructions. They don't know what else to do, nor do they care if we make mistakes when entering the information.

There is a saying in the computer field which goes, "Garbage In, Garbage Out." This means that if you fill up your computer's memory with useless or incorrect information, that is exactly what you will get out of it when you retrieve it. There's no point in getting upset with your computer, because it only does what it's been told to do. Imagine, for a moment, a computer that was programmed in an entirely negative way. Let's suppose that every time you punched a key, the computer was programmed to flash the following message onto the screen: "Sorry, Fatso, I am unable to perform to my potential." No matter what you were trying to do, the same frustrating message would appear. Now imagine someone trying to use this computer to calculate a complex problem. Try as she might, nothing would happen. The same negative message would continue to show up on the screen. The fact is, unless the machine were reprogrammed to do something different, the message would continue to repeat itself over and over again. This is because the computer doesn't know any other way to respond. All it has ever been shown to do is to create the message it is spitting out.

Unfortunately, most of us have programmed *ourselves* in a very similar manner. We are literally living with a "Garbage In, Garbage Out" mind-set and wondering why we are dissatisfied with our lives. We have been giving ourselves the types of messages (or programming) that prohibits us from succeeding at our goals and becoming happy and successful with our lives. We have created beliefs about ourselves by our own verbal "programming." We have been telling ourselves over and over again how we feel about ourselves and how we wish ourselves to perform. If these messages have been primarily negative in nature, is it any wonder that we experience failure or frustration? Unfortunately, in terms of our attitudes about our weight, many of us have reinforced the belief, "Sorry, Fatso, I am unable to perform to my potential."

What most of us forget is that **WE ARE THE PROGRAMMERS** of our own minds. Although we hear suggestions and comments from others, ultimately our belief systems can be traced back to the types of messages we offer to our subconscious minds.

You may feel very strongly that "I'm a good cook," "I'm a good mother/father," or "I'm very easygoing." The reason you are these things (or anything else) is because you believe them to be true. You believe them to be true because you are constantly reinforcing the fact with your verbal and mental messages. Over time, you have convinced yourself that these characteristics are simply part of you. You have "programmed" your mind to assume you have these qualities. Because you tell yourself they are true, they become so.

Anything about ourselves which we believe to be negative is also due to our own negative programming. For example, every time you tell yourself that you're "a very fast eater," or that you "love to eat fast food," you are actively programming your mind to accept these characteristics as *truth*. So when you look in the mirror you will see a person who is, for example, five feet six inches tall, blonde, blue-eyed, and who eats fast food very quickly. When looked at in this way, you can see how silly it is to program yourself in this manner. Instead of looking at yourself as "someone who eats fast food very quickly," why not program yourself to be someone who takes time to enjoy her food and who eats only when she's hungry?

Fortunately, we do have the ability to "reprogram" *any* negative perception or attitude that we have about ourselves. The most effective means of doing so is by using positive thoughts and affirmations, such as: **"I eat very slowly and enjoy my food"** to reestablish control over our own thinking process. If practiced with enthusiasm and persistency, statements like these can replace the old ones as the "truisms" for us. As our mental perception of ourselves is changed, our behavior will change accordingly. As you become more familiar with positive beliefs about yourself, you will see how easily this process can work. Our beliefs are the result of what we tell ourselves and what we accept as true. As we first become consciously aware of what we are saying to ourselves, and secondly reprogram our minds with new, more productive replacement messages, our bodies will respond with enjoyment and delight.

With this in mind, let's practice the affirmation for this chapter. Repeat this phrase to yourself slowly with a great deal of enthusiasm three times:

---

## I EAT SLOWLY AND ENJOY MY FOOD

◆

## I EAT SLOWLY AND ENJOY MY FOOD

◆

## I EAT SLOWLY AND ENJOY MY FOOD

---

Rather than thinking about how quickly you finish your meals, begin to notice the *intervals between your bites*. This will take your attention off how fast you eat and put it on how slowly you eat. Now, repeat once again:

---

## I EAT VERY SLOWLY AND ENJOY MY FOOD

---

Practice this affirmation frequently throughout the day. It becomes particularly powerful when you think of it either right before or during a meal. This affirmation is a good one to demonstrate the *direct relationship* between your words and your actions. It shows you how the simple act of acknowledging a positive quality in yourself can encourage that quality to exist and develop.

EXERCISE

# 15A

The exercise for this chapter is very useful in the area of reprogramming our subconscious minds. It's a lot of fun and I encourage you to practice it often. The goal of this exercise is to completely eliminate any negative messages that exist in your subconscious mind on the subjects of food and eating.

We are going to imagine that your mind is an actual physical computer system and your job is to reprogram it. The first step is to determine what information is already existing in your memory.

Pull out a piece of paper and begin to write down any negative messages you can think of that you give to yourself on the subjects of food and eating. Be creative and think of as many negative messages as you can. Here is a small sample of what someone's list may look like:

I ALWAYS GAIN WEIGHT DURING THE HOLIDAYS.
I CAN'T GO WITHOUT DESSERT.
I'VE ALWAYS HATED TO EXERCISE.
I'VE ALWAYS EATEN TOO MUCH.
I LOVE FATTY FOODS LIKE BUTTER AND CHEESE.
BEING OVERWEIGHT RUNS IN MY FAMILY.
DIETS DON'T WORK.
IT'S SO HARD TO LOSE WEIGHT.
EXERCISE IS BORING.

This is only a sample of the literally hundreds of possibilities. Each person's list will be unique and different in length. After you're convinced that your list is complete you are ready for step two.

Step two involves creating a separate "replacement" affirmation for each of the statements you have written down. So, if you have twenty negative messages to contend with, you will need an equal number of replacements. Each new affirmation you create should be tailored to the negative message you are attempting to eliminate. For example, let's look at the first three messages in our list above. Statement number one reads: "I always gain weight during the holidays." You want to create an affirmation that will turn this useless, negative belief about yourself into a productive belief that can help you control your weight. Thus, for statement number one, you might use the affirmation

## THE HOLIDAYS ARE A TIME WHERE MY WILL-POWER IS PARTICULARLY STRONG

This affirmation keeps your attention on the holidays but turns a negative statement into a positive one. Now, instead of setting yourself up and reminding yourself that you must overeat every time you go to a holiday party, you are setting the stage to enjoy the affair, knowing that you are in complete control of your eating. You will be pleasantly surprised to discover that, as this message is entered into your subconscious mind, you will find it much easier to refrain from overeating at parties. The mere act of practicing affirmations such as these reminds you of your goal when the situation is called for.

The second statement reads, "I can't go without dessert." This statement suggests to and reminds your subconscious mind that you crave sweets or dessert after meals. By this time you are probably beginning to see that this statement is nothing more than a programmed belief about yourself that needs to be changed. Why keep reminding yourself of something that is counterproductive to your needs and to your health? Instead, you need to replace this belief about yourself with a new one, suggesting that you are sufficiently satisfied after finishing meals. You need to start believing that you not only don't need dessert but don't even want it. With this in mind, you might come up with a "replacement" affirmation such as

## A CUP OF TEA AFTER DINNER IS A WONDERFUL WAY TO COMPLEMENT MY MEAL; IT'S ALL I NEED

Once you start believing this, you will see that it's relatively simple to replace "dessert" with something like a cup of tea or even a glass of water. Again, the only reason you think you need dessert is because you have programmed yourself to believe that you do. Each time you tell yourself that you need it, you are reinforcing the very belief you would like to change.

Statement number three reads, "I've always hated to exercise." How in the world are you going to get excited about walking or jogging around the city park, or any other type of exercise, with this type of belief system? Quite frankly, it's not very likely. This message suggests boredom, work, and loathing around the very thought of exercising your body. Again, talking about and reminding yourself about your dislike for exercise will only reinforce the certainty of your position. Instead, be kind to yourself. Practice giving yourself gentle suggestions that there *are* exercises that can be enjoyable to you (see chapter 10). It would serve your purposes better to replace this negative message about exercise with the affirmation

## THERE IS AN EXERCISE THAT IS PERFECT FOR ME: IT IS . . .

You fill in the blank.

Continue with this procedure by going through your entire list in a similar manner. Spend some thought on each "replacement affirmation," then go on to part three.

Part three is a visualization exercise. Refer to chapter 4 if you need to refresh your memory on the key aspects of this important topic.

The visualization portion of this exercise is tremendously effective when practiced alone or with a friend. Sometimes having a partner can be helpful because he or she can guide you through the process. If you are alone, utilize the technique discussed in chapter 4 which involves reading the exercise into a tape recorder and playing it back to yourself.

You are now ready to begin the process of "reprogramming" your mind to accept your new messages. Before doing so, however, you will want to remove the old messages that are stored in your memory.

Start by closing your eyes and getting yourself into a very relaxed state. Remember that visualization exercises are most effective when all other thoughts are allowed to drift from your mind and when your body and mind are very relaxed. Take yourself through the relaxation procedure, which allows you to be as comfortable and relaxed as possible.

With your eyes closed and your body very relaxed, picture the words of your first negative affirmation in your "mind's eye." If you were using the list we referred to earlier, your picture would be the words, "I always gain weight during the holidays." Whatever *your* message is, picture it clearly in your mind's eye for fifteen to thirty seconds.

Remember that you are thinking of your mind as a computer system. Keeping your eyes closed, imagine the screen of a computer right before your eyes. If you are unfamiliar with what a computer looks like, simply imagine a television screen instead; the two are very similar. Now, see the words you are imagining in your mind as if they were on the screen. The screen will act as your imaginary computer.

Computers are equipped with a "backspace" or "erase" key, which can permanently erase anything on your screen if you wish it to disappear. You simply locate what you wish to erase, then push the desired button—it's that simple! The message will be erased from the computer's memory, which is then ready for new information.

Remember that you have programmed your mind just like a computer. The information has been entered via your words and thoughts and is now waiting for further instructions.

Next, imagine that there is a button on the bottom right corner of your screen. The button is round and black, and on it is the word "erase." Whenever you push the black button, everything on your screen will be erased, not only from the screen but also completely out of your memory as well. In other words, once the information is erased, it will no longer be part of you. With this in mind, take one final look at the words on your screen and wish them good-bye. When you are ready, push the button and watch the words vanish!

The most effective way to proceed is to work with one replacement at a time. In other words, rather than going through and erasing all the negative messages from your "computer" at once, erase one negative message at a time and replace it with your selected replacement affirmation.

Another component of the computer you will want to be aware of is the keyboard. This is the part of the computer, similar to a typewriter, that allows you to type in new information. If you are comfortable imagining a typewriter, great, if not, simply imagine a pencil, and you will print the new information onto your screen. Both ways are equally effective for this exercise. As always with affirmation and visualization exercises, choose the one that feels best to you.

Now imagine yourself, in your mind's eye, typing (or printing) the replacement affirmation onto your screen. Remember to use the affirmation you have specifically chosen for the message you have just eliminated from your memory. In the example we are using, you would type or print the words

### THE HOLIDAYS ARE A TIME WHEN MY WILL-POWER IS PARTICULARLY STRONG

Type or print the words in large, all capital, bold letters. This will allow for the greatest impact on your subconscious mind.

After typing or printing your unique message, take fifteen or thirty seconds to carefully examine what you have just written. Really take in the information and remember that this message is going to be a permanent part of your thinking process.

Right next to the black (erase) button on the bottom right corner of your screen, you will find a bright red button, which is a little larger than the other. Picture this button in your mind right now. Notice that inside the button is the word, "SAVE."

Know that once you push this button, the information on your screen is there to stay, forever, unless you go through the procedure for erasing it. Your new message will replace your old one as part of your personal "truth." Now, as you are looking at your *new* message, push the "SAVE" button to put the message into your memory permanently!

Go through this procedure for each one of your matched pairs of affirmations. It's best to practice only a couple of pairs in a single session so that you can offer the exercise your full attention.

Anytime you catch yourself giving yourself a negative message about food or eating is a good time to practice this exercise. The more times you do it, the less often the old messages will come up in your mind or in your conversation. The goal is to see yourself eventually as someone who doesn't have any of the negative characteristics you are wishing to eliminate.

This exercise is very effective and powerful. Anytime you hear yourself, or anyone else, offering you a negative, self-defeating message, there is an element of "programming" going on. The idea behind exercises such as this is to become consciously aware of the programming taking place. By becoming consciously involved in the process, you become empowered, rather than victimized by your own words and those of others.

# 16

## Acting as Your Own Authority

◆

**Y**ou will always hear reasons why "Dieting and hard work are the only ways to lose weight," why, "It takes a long time to lose weight," and "You should never eat this or that food." As long as you accept these and similar negative statements as *absolute truth*, you are trapped; you are literally a prisoner of other people's reality structure because you have let "other people" decide for you how you are going to go about losing weight. If you decide in advance that something isn't going to work for you just because everyone else says it isn't going to, then you are letting other people act as your "authority figure."

Affirmations, visualizations, meditations, mental exercises, and the like are quite different from "external" methods of weight control. They are all vehicles to tap into your innate bodily wisdom, which intuitively knows exactly how much you should weigh and just how to go about achieving this optimal weight. It's time to select the method that **you** decide is going to work for **you**.

One of my favorite sayings comes from Richard Bach's beautiful book *Illusions*, where it is said, "Argue for your limitations and they're yours." I believe that almost nothing in the world is so true. So much emphasis in our lives is put on all the excuses and reasons we cannot do certain things. It's almost as though we hang on to, defend, and yes, even "argue" for our own limitations. People tell us it's hard to lose weight, so we believe them. They tell us "exercise is boring," so we think it is so.

Think for a minute about all the reasons why it's "hard to lose weight," all the reasons you could "put it off," and why "it's going to take a long time to achieve." If you are able to take a step back, and think philosophically about it, I'm convinced you will find that these types of thoughts and negative affirmations about weight loss are just what they sound like: obstacles and habits that need to be eliminated. Instead of telling yourself how difficult it's going to be, change your affirmation to: *"I love taking care of my body; it's a privilege."* Then, using various types of inner disciplines, find ways to make the affirmation a truism in your life. Repeat this message to yourself with love and meaning at least three times, right now.

---

I LOVE TAKING CARE OF MY BODY; IT'S A PRIVILEGE

◆

I LOVE TAKING CARE OF MY BODY; IT'S A PRIVILEGE

◆

I LOVE TAKING CARE OF MY BODY; IT'S A PRIVILEGE

---

Repeat this affirmation several times throughout the day. You will have changed a negative, self-defeating message, which does no good whatsoever, to a positive message, which inspires, encourages, and assists you in losing weight and in taking care of your body. Give yourself frequent, positive messages about your new way of taking care of yourself. When you take care of yourself, your body treats you wonderfully. You'll have tremendous amounts of energy, you'll feel great, and you'll be proud to look in the mirror.

Excuses, negative conversation, and negative affirmations to ourselves only serve to defeat us. The patterns in our lives are never improved due to negativity or negative affirmations. Things simply continue on as they are, or get even worse, because of them.

A typical pattern in many people's diets, or efforts at weight loss goes something like this. They tell themselves over and over again that eating pizza (or any number of other examples) is going to make them fat. The fact that they are talking so much about the food reminds them how much they think they enjoy it. Eventually, because so much attention and energy is focused on the food they are thinking about, they "break down" and "treat" themselves to a pizza. After finishing their meal, they tell themselves, "I shouldn't have done that," and proceed to burden themselves with guilt and remorse, thus reinforcing once again that they will surely gain weight from eating the pizza. After going home, or the next morning, they weigh themselves, and sure enough they have gained a pound. "See, I knew it," they'll say, thus reinforcing, yet another time, how eating something they enjoy makes them gain weight.

People almost never consider the possibility that their negative thoughts about food are contributing to their weight gain. They automatically assume that it was only the "pizza" that did it. After all, doesn't everyone tell them, "Pizza is fattening" and "If you eat pizza, you'll surely gain weight"? The truth is that it wasn't *only* the pizza that made them gain the weight. Sure, the pizza contained the necessary calories, but it was all the focus, attention, and negative thought forms that went into the pizza that made them eat it in the first place. I'm not suggesting that pizza isn't fattening. I am, however, suggesting that if people were to learn some very simple meditation and visualization exercises, they could *absolutely* control their desire for certain foods, *100 percent of the time!* Inner control creates outer discipline, not the other way around as "diets" suggest. Willpower does *not* come from forcing yourself to do certain things, it comes from a quiet, non-agitated mind. With inner work you don't have to force yourself to do anything. By learning and practicing various types of mental exercises (that is, the practice exercises at the end of each chapter), you can simply allow your body to take over.

Being your own authority means deciding for *yourself* what is, and is not, good for you. Critics will invariably misinterpret the meaning of "being your own authority" by saying such things as: "If you think I can eat *only* chocolate and I can continue to maintain not only my weight, but my health as well, you're crazy!" I can only say that people who make these types of comments are not being their own authority at all. In fact I've never met a single person who "acted as her own authority" who also chose to eat chocolate all of the time. The fact of the matter is that as you start to decide for yourself what you *really* want to eat, you begin to eat healthier food, not the other way around. I'm not saying you can "eat only chocolate and still lose weight," I *am* saying that if you truly act as *your own authority* you will rise above the advertisers' claims that chocolate (or anything else) tastes great and should be looked on as a treat. Your inner wisdom will help you decide where and when you will eat chocolate, if at all. You will decide for yourself whether or not you even think chocolate tastes good. You will **not** be influenced by your friends, family, or anyone else. If others are going out for ice cream, you will not eat it *simply* because everyone else is doing so. You will eat it if, and only if, you *choose* to eat it. You will learn to "fine tune" your awareness of what your body really wants. Eventually you will be able to close your eyes, go deep within yourself, and find out in a matter of seconds what you feel like eating.

Being your own authority means much more than deciding for yourself when you will eat a certain food. It also means you will decide for yourself when and if you are hungry at all. Where did we ever get the idea that eating "three square meals per day" was a positive or even a "necessary" thing to do? What do you suppose would happen to the restaurant and food industry if everyone in America decided that from now on they were going to eat only one meal per day? Obviously, there are a lot of people and industries with a financial interest in keeping people stuck in their overeating habits. I'm not suggesting that you necessarily eat only one meal per day, but I'm also not suggesting that you eat three meals a day, or more. That is, unless **you** decide that is what **you** feel is best for **you**. Personally, I sometimes eat one meal a day, sometimes three, and sometimes none at all. I have no rules for myself other than an attempt to be *my own authority* at all times. The way I act as my own authority is by going "inside myself," closing my eyes, and doing a very short meditation exercise. I gently ask myself what I would really like to eat, and approximately how much. We will practice this type of meditation at the end of this chapter.

Virtually every diet book I have ever seen contains elaborate lists of all the items you should and should not eat. Some of them even tell you what time you should eat and what brand you should buy. I don't know about you, but it gets pretty complicated for me! To participate in such programs, it seems that you have to either have a photographic memory or carry around charts and lists of what it is okay to eat. What if you could learn to decide for *yourself* what you were to eat, when you would do so, and how much you needed? The only rationale for letting others decide these things for you is that you somehow believe that others know better than you do what it is you need. Once you become your *own* authority by trusting your inner voice, I believe you will feel, as I do, that this is an absurd assumption.

This is not a prescription for eating food that is not good for you or for eating too much. I believe that if you sit down and go inside yourself, you will find that you already know what you need. You certainly don't need long lists of exactly what foods to eat and when to eat them. Most diets put so much attention on food that it's difficult to think of anything else. By becoming your own authority, you place less emphasis on food and more emphasis on how you really feel. The focal point is on turning inward to find out what it is you want.

In addition to deciding what, how much, and when you choose to eat, your inner voice will help you decide what foods *will do what* for your body. That's right: *you decide*! As long as you let others tell you what your body needs to make it slender, it's more difficult to trust your inner self. If you decide, with a quiet mind, that a certain food is what you need to bring your body satisfaction, then you need to decide to eat it. For example, let's suppose you are craving a dish of pasta for dinner. If your inner wisdom tells you that if you eat the pasta, you will be satisfied, you'll be happy about your decision, and the food will bring you nutrition, energy, and vitality that can be used to maintain your strength, then EAT IT! You will find that after eating a meal that you **feel good about,** you will have more energy for exercise and more enthusiasm for losing weight. Most importantly, you will be inclined to give yourself positive, thankful affirmations about what the pasta is doing to your body. Compare this alternative to looking in your latest fad diet book and finding out that on Tuesday evenings you are to eat four ounces of beef, a small salad, and a half serving of rice. In this example, *someone else* has decided what, how much, and when you are going to eat. Suppose you resent (even a little bit) the fact that you have to eat beef tonight, because first of all you don't even like it, and secondly you know very well that your body is craving something different. What types of messages are you likely to give yourself if you force yourself to eat something that you don't really want? You may find yourself saying things to yourself such as, "See, this diet is hard and I must sacrifice to lose weight." If this were the case, you would have once again affirmed to yourself that (1) diets are hard, (2) you need willpower to lose weight, and (3) you probably won't get much energy or enjoyment out of the food. How can that type of thought process possibly be helpful? It all seems to be pretty complicated! Wouldn't a simpler alternative be to learn to go inward and trust the answers that present themselves?

This brings us to our next affirmation. Remember the important elements of affirmations, especially the part about enthusiasm! Repeat this affirmation either out loud or to yourself, and *really mean it.* Repeat the statement three times.

I AM MY OWN AUTHORITY

◆

I AM MY OWN AUTHORITY

◆

I AM MY OWN AUTHORITY

Once again, remember to repeat the message like you really mean it! If you feel that you need to, say it again. Keep repeating this affirmation until you believe it so strongly that you can't imagine it any other way. This is one of the most important affirmations in this book because it affirms that you are in charge of your own destiny. Your weight is in *your own hands*. You are telling yourself that you are not a dietary victim. Rather, you are giving yourself the positive suggestion that you trust your own inner resources.

The last two affirmations for this chapter are very closely related and should be practiced together. They are:

---

# I MAKE MY OWN DECISIONS ABOUT FOOD
## AND
# I EAT ONLY WHEN I'M HUNGRY

---

Now, repeat both statements again, three times, like you really believe them. Think carefully about what you are saying. The words in these affirmations are very powerful. They suggest that your decisions about food are important and that you are in charge of those decisions.

---

# I MAKE MY OWN DECISIONS ABOUT FOOD
## AND
# I EAT ONLY WHEN I'M HUNGRY

◆

# I MAKE MY OWN DECISIONS ABOUT FOOD
## AND
# I EAT ONLY WHEN I'M HUNGRY

◆

# I MAKE MY OWN DECISIONS ABOUT FOOD
## AND
# I EAT ONLY WHEN I'M HUNGRY!

---

When we were children, we instinctively ate only when we were hungry. Many of us learned as we were growing up, however, that "not eating" was considered the same as "not feeling well." Our parents, grandparents, or other authority figures would make comments like, "You'd better eat if you want to grow up to be a big, strong man like Daddy," or "Oh my gosh! Sara isn't eating—she must not be feeling well." We learned that, in order to gain approval, we had to eat everything on our plate. We learned that we were disappointing those people we loved most if we did not eat.

The need for approval in our lives is based on one simple premise; namely, don't trust yourself; trust others to make your decisions for you. Now ask yourself this question:

**Do I want to let others make my decisions for me or would I rather make them for myself?**

My guess is that you answered the question by stating, "Of course I want to make my own choices." Remember, however, that certain choices that we make are unconscious in nature. Again, this means that there is a part of our minds that makes decisions, or does certain things, without other parts of us even knowing about it. We might finish our dinner, eating long after we feel full, because we unconsciously want to please our mother, our father, or grandma. It's easy to see how overeating habits develop. If approval is important to you, and you feel (even at an unconscious level) that you are getting approval for overeating, you will have little reason to want to change your behavior. The best way to eliminate these unconscious motivators from your life is to continue to do positive affirmations and other types of inner work.

You can love and respect your parents and grandparents without overeating. In fact, you will probably love them more than ever because you will let go of any unconscious anger you may have toward them for contributing to your subconscious negative beliefs about food. As you become more and more in charge of your own decisions about food, especially your unconscious ones, you may find other people coming to you for approval and/or mimicking your eating habits. This is because you will probably be the only person on the block who is not eating out of pure habit but rather out of your own inner resources and needs. Of course, the goal is **not** to have others seeking your approval. This is just as much a trap as seeking approval yourself. If you find others doing so, simply encourage them, as you have learned, to trust themselves, not you. **Leave trusting you . . . to you.**

## EXERCISE
# 16A

This exercise should be done ten minutes before your next meal and thereafter before every meal if possible.

Find a place where you are sure you can be alone for a period of five to ten minutes. Allow yourself to get into a very comfortable position, either lying down or sitting in a comfortable chair. Take a moment to loosen any restrictive clothing, especially around your waist and neck.

Begin by taking ten very deep and slow breaths. Allow the oxygen to flow evenly and deeply into your lungs. With each exhalation, feel the tension in your body release completely. Allow yourself to relax. Let your shoulders go, let go of your jaw, your neck, and your shoulders. Feel your lungs expanding, then letting go, expanding, then letting go again.

Now, take a few moments to connect with your "inner guide," or "inner advisor" as you learned in chapter 5. If it seems easier, just prepare to ask yourself a simple question. However you decide to do it, allow the answers to come to your mind. Let all extraneous thoughts flow from your mind. There is just you and your breath relaxing together, deeply and quietly.

Once you feel completely relaxed, ask yourself or your "inner guide," what and how much food you feel you truly want and need for the upcoming meal. Remind yourself that you wish to eliminate any food that is desired because of anxiety, tiredness, agitation, anger, fear, or pure reaction. You want your inner wisdom to let you know exactly how much food you need when all the usual factors are taken away. A relaxed body and mind almost always needs far less food than an anxious one.

Keep in mind that one of the major purposes to this exercise is to work on "being your own authority." This means deciding in advance how much you really feel like eating, even if it means disappointing someone else who may have made the meal for you. Sometimes people want *you* to eat too much so that *they* can feel okay about eating a lot themselves. People can apply unconscious pressure on you to get you to be more like them. There is no need to be upset at anyone, but rather it's simply helpful if you know of this tendency in advance. The purpose of this exercise is to remind yourself that you're in charge of your own decisions, period.

Give your mind and higher self plenty of time to respond to your questions of what and how much you really want to eat. While you're waiting, take a few more deep, relaxing breaths, knowing that the answers will come in their own time. The answer you receive may come in the form of a voice, a sound, or a picture. The form it takes is not important. What *is* important is that you begin to sense that inner part of yourself that only you can access. It's for this reason that you *have* to be your own authority. Listen carefully for the answer that comes. You will be given, at the very least, a clue as to what and how much to eat. Ideally, the specifics will be very clear.

All decisions about what and how much to eat should be made with a quiet mind in a similar manner. Eventually, you'll be able to do this exercise in a matter of seconds right before sitting down to a meal. You are training yourself to tune inward, rather than outward, to meet your body's nutritional needs.

# 17

◆ ══════════ ◆

# The Ten Commandments

◆

Almost everyone has heard of the ten commandments. They are, of course, guidelines
for moral and loving living. Because affirmations
are, in a sense, commandments to ourselves, let's
outline ten of the most essential messages we wish
to master. This entire chapter can be thought of as
an exercise of affirmations. Some have been mentioned already, and some have not. They are ten of
the most important messages you can possibly get
in the habit of giving yourself.

As always, remember the essential elements of
successful affirmations. Practice the messages with
meaning and determination, using either the "prac-

tice" or the "active" method. Practice them frequently with the idea that you are already succeeding. Feel free to refer to chapter 3 if you need to refresh your memory about additional important practice information.

# 1

## I AM MY OWN AUTHORITY

This affirmation remains one of the most important of all. It sets the stage for all the others to become effective. In order to get the most out of your affirmations, you must be completely in charge of your own life. You alone need to decide which messages you want to send to your subconscious mind and how you wish to treat your body.

# 2

## I LOVE MYSELF AND MY BODY

This affirmation has several meanings. First, it suggests a separateness between your consciousness and your body. You are not only a physical body but a pure state of consciousness as well. This is important, because your consciousness understands even more than your body that it creates its own reality through the messages it receives. It knows that the body will change as the messages it receives are changed. In addition, this affirmation suggests that you care enough about your body to take charge of your health and your weight.

◆ ═══ ◆

## 3

## I REPLACE EVERY NEGATIVE AFFIRMATION WITH A POSITIVE ONE

This affirmation is about taking charge of your own life and creating your own affirmations. It encourages you to look at *every* message you give to yourself. As you notice a negative message *of any kind* creeping into your vocabulary, you will instantly catch it and create a positive affirmation to take its place. This is an important affirmation to master after finishing this book, because you will want to develop your own affirmations to supplement the ones you have learned here.

◆ ══════ ◆

# 4

## I LOVE HEALTHY FOOD

We looked at this affirmation earlier. Its message speaks for itself. As you constantly remind yourself of the fact that you love healthy food, you will naturally seek out this type of nourishment. As this message becomes more and more a part of your life, you will notice yourself avoiding anything that does not fit into this category. As you understand more and more completely how much you love healthy food, both your energy and the quality of your life will be enhanced.

# 5

## VITALITY IS MY NATURAL STATE

This message reminds your subconscious mind of what your body wants to feel like. Your body knows that healthy food gives it energy and life force. This message reminds you that to feel good is to feel alive. This message reinforces the previous affirmation because, in order to have the greatest degree of vitality, you need to understand the connection between vitality and healthy food.

◆ ═══ ◆

# 6

## MY LIFE IS EASY AND I AM CAPABLE OF ANYTHING

We have seen the importance of eliminating all negative messages from our vocabulary and from our subconscious minds. This begins with the messages we give to ourselves about our life in general. As long as we believe that "life is hard," so it will be. This will include any attempt to diet or lose weight. Nothing is difficult unless you first convince yourself that it is. This affirmation will affirm the value of seeing life and everything in it (including weight loss) as easy.

◆ ═══ ◆

# 7

## MY APPETITE IS SMALL AND I ONLY EAT WHEN I'M HUNGRY

Your appetite is exactly the same size as you think it is. Thus, as far as losing weight goes, almost nothing is more important than the belief you have about the size of your appetite. In an earlier chapter, we discussed how the size of your appetite came about. You were not born with a preset appetite but rather developed it over time. This affirmation retrains your subconscious mind about a belief that can easily be changed. With practice, especially just before you sit down to eat, you may notice an almost instant shift in the amount of food you feel you need to eat. This affirmation also suggests to your subconscious mind that you alone decide when to eat. You no longer eat simply because it's breakfast, lunch, or dinner time. Similarly, you no longer eat simply because others are doing so. This includes your friends and even your family. You can be with others while they're eating without feeling obligated to do the same. Remember that you are your own authority! This message also suggests that you make conscious, caring choices about your body and its needs. Your body wants you to "tune in" to when it needs food, not to eat simply out of habit.

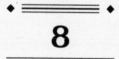

# 8

## I CAN ALWAYS EAT LATER IF I'M STILL HUNGRY

This affirmation takes the panic out of "not getting enough food." It reminds you that you don't have to eat it all right now. This affirmation reduces the fears that may have developed in early childhood. Once you're convinced that you can always eat later, you'll drop the need to eat everything on your plate.

As was true with the last affirmation, this is very effective if practiced directly before sitting down to eat.

◆ ══ ◆

# 9

## IT IS THROUGH MY FORGIVENESS THAT I LOVE MYSELF: THE MORE I LOVE MYSELF THE MORE I WILL CARE FOR MY BODY

Forgiveness is the secret to successful living. Forgive yourself right now for anything, and everything, you have ever done. Give yourself the message that you are okay just the way you are. You do not need to change to be loved by yourself or by anyone else. If you wish to change, however, forgiveness is the only answer. An unforgiving mind is stuck in its way of thinking and is thus incapable of change. Forgiveness offers your subconscious mind the message that you are both worthy and capable of achieving anything you desire. Remember that all criticism is counterproductive and, in a sense, a waste of energy. Forgiveness is the key to change. Practice this affirmation often; it can change your life.

The last commandment is the most important one you can ever learn, and there is a special way to go about practicing it. Go to a mirror and look into your eyes. Don't just glance, but really look to see who's inside. Look very carefully at the person before you. Spend several minutes just looking. Now repeat the affirmation:

◆ ══ ◆

# 10

## I LOVE YOU    I LOVE YOU    I LOVE YOU

This affirmation and exercise should be practiced every morning upon waking and every evening before going to bed. Make it a regular part of your life. It could be the most important, most life-changing event you ever take part in. Loving ourselves is an art and a skill. Most people spend far more time cleaning their cars than they do telling themselves they are lovable. As loving yourself becomes a top priority, you will notice remarkable changes occurring in your life. If you practiced only one affirmation, this would be the one. Practice it often, and enjoy your life!

There is one very important point to keep in mind while learning and practicing these as well as each of the other affirmations contained in this book. While these affirmations are very effective and capable of producing lasting and profound changes, they are only the beginning. I encourage you to try each of them, keeping in mind that you can create your own. If these work, great! Use them to your heart's content. There is value, however, in creating your own affirmations based on your own set of needs. Each person is unique and special. Individual differences and preferences should be taken into account and honored. Remember commandment number (1) which says, "I am my own authority." You may decide to use the affirmations in this book, or you may decide to use your own, or both. It's up to you!

# Be Good to Yourself!

# 18

❖ ═══════════ ❖

# Getting Support

❖

While the emphasis of this book is on "inner empowerment," you should never think that seeking the support of others is inconsistent with this goal. In fact, sharing your predicament with other caring individuals is one of the most powerful tools for successful inner development and growth. This is because sharing encourages you to search deeper within yourself than is sometimes possible alone. Sharing encourages self-honesty, introspection, and self-love by allowing you to be clearer about your motivations, fears, and feelings.

Many of us have experienced times when we use food as a way to avoid dealing with our true feelings. When we feel anxious, it's often easier to reach for food than it is to confront an uncomfortable feeling. What "support from others" offers us is the recognition that we are not alone in our feelings. Whether support comes from an organized overeaters' group, a private session with a qualified therapist, or simply the love of a trusted friend, seeking support is *always* a good idea.

Many people feel embarrassed, ashamed, or simply too scared to share their feelings about their weight with others. I've heard people say, "Even if I did seek help, what good could it do anyway?" Those same people are often the ones who later report that "Seeking outside support was the most important thing I ever did for myself."

Some of us are blessed with partners, family members, or close friends who can act as a source of support for us. Unfortunately, some of us are not so lucky. This does not suggest that our family and friends are not good people. There are many loving and caring people who simply *don't understand* what it's like to have an issue with their weight. It's in these cases that seeking outside intervention becomes even more important. A good example of this comes from an acquaintance of mine who, several years ago, lost more than 100 pounds over a period of fifteen months. His wife, in an attempt to "prepare him for disappointment," kept reminding him of how "unlikely" it was that he would keep the weight off. She was constantly referring to his past failed attempts, both to him and to their mutual friends. Eventually, he lost his confidence and gained back all the weight. Clearly, the ultimate responsibility to keep the weight off has to fall on the person losing the weight. We can't blame others, nor can we assume that other people are even partly responsible for giving us the encouragement we need. Despite this recognition, however, we can see how this type of behavior is unhelpful, if not detrimental, to our attempts to lose weight. In the case of my acquaintance, his wife was doing what she felt was best for him. I'm sure she didn't consciously want her husband to gain the weight back that he had worked so hard to lose. Instead, she was simply unaware that her constant reminders that he was destined to fail were powerful negative messages that may have had an impact on his confidence and long-term results. There's no way to tell whether or not positive reinforcement would have had an effect on his confidence and results, but I suspect that it might have. In any case, I strongly believe that had he added some sort of external source of support to his already effective weight-loss program, he would have quite easily kept the weight off to this present day.

Many human potential, addiction, and problem-solving agencies recognize the importance of sharing our experience and feelings with others. Whether it be a fear of public speaking, a fear of heights, substance abuse, a fear of flying, or issues of eating and weight control, most legitimate professionals advocate the use of support groups as part of their treatment programs. It's a beautiful part of human nature to have the desire to share our feelings, and hear those of others, about issues of importance in our lives.

It has been shown that overeating is sometimes used to fill a "void" in our lives. Many times, this void is an inner emptiness that comes about from believing that "no one understands me." Food then becomes the substitute for the understanding we are searching for. So often what happens when people join a support group is that, perhaps for the first time in their lives, they see and feel that they are not alone. They see that everyone in the group feels very much the same way they do. They have many of the same desires, the same fears, the same motivations, and the same feelings. This is equally true for *all* types of addictions whether it be alcohol, coffee, cigarettes, hard drugs, or food. Obviously, we are all human beings. What people in support groups discover, however, is that they are human beings who share the same predicament. All of us have feelings, concerns, and questions about our lives. None of us is perfect!

Many people find that, as they are listened to and understood by others going through the same process, it becomes much easier to work through their weight problems. They find that the inner emptiness they had was due, at least in part, to "not being listened to," or "fully understood." As they find the support they were lacking, recovery becomes a greater possibility.

In addition to sharing our feelings, listening to others is an extremely important part of support. In addition to discovering that we're not alone, we can also begin, through other people's sharing, to gain some insight into our own problems. Someone may be sharing a feeling or telling a story that sparks the thought in us, "That's me." In this respect other people become a sort of "mirror" for us, reflecting parts of ourselves that we may be unfamiliar with or that we might not have wanted to look at. Either way, the value is there. Anytime we have the chance to see additional aspects of ourselves, we should jump at the opportunity. Remember that much of this book deals with bringing to our consciousness that which is unconscious. Once a feeling or emotion is acknowledged, it creates new options in our lives. Once we are aware of a feeling, we can decide what, if anything, needs to be done. As long as an emotion or feeling is buried inside ourselves, or hidden from our consciousness, it can run our lives without our even knowing it.

Finally, I'd like to point out that seeking outside help is *not*, in any way, reserved for people who are obese or greatly overweight. Weight issues are very individual. If you think of yourself as five pounds overweight, seeking support is just as important as if you think of yourself as seventy-five pounds overweight. In fact, if you're not overweight at all but would simply like to be able to feel better about your present weight or about yourself in gen-

eral, seeking support will still be tremendously helpful. Ultimately, each of us would like to feel as
positive about ourselves as possible. This means
eliminating our self-criticism, reducing as many of
our fears as possible, and learning to love and understand ourselves in a very deep way. Seeking support
will oftentimes help us achieve these results much
quicker than if we go it alone.

EXERCISE

## 18A

It should come as no surprise that the object of this
exercise is to begin to share your feelings with
others. There is no set way to do this exercise; the
method is up to you. Very simply, the object is to
find a close friend, relative, spouse, or outside
therapist to talk to about your feelings. The important thing is that you trust the person you choose.
The specific feelings you talk about are for you to
decide. You can talk about "how you feel" when you
don't get enough to eat or how you feel when you
eat too much. You can talk about what it's like to be
overweight or to feel that food is too big of an issue

in your life. Anything and everything is fair game, as long as the conversation gets into your feelings about your weight and your self-image.

What tends to happen when people do this exercise is that they begin to notice how the person they are sharing with begins to open up too. While it's very nice when others open to us, the key to this exercise is to get practice in opening up ourselves. While most of us are open at times, this exercise is attempting to get you to go a little deeper than you might be accustomed to. Really make an attempt to "stretch" yourself in being open. Stretching allows for insight and growth. See if, in sharing, you are able to learn something *new* about yourself—something that you didn't already know. Remember that each new insight you have about yourself and your feelings is bringing up aspects of your consciousness that you may not have been aware of. Sharing is the most effective way to allow this consciousness to surface.

# 19

## Forgiveness

An essential element of all inner work is the quality of forgiveness. Forgiveness means letting go of the past and of our negative misperceptions of ourselves.

One of the primary objectives of inner work is to replace old negative messages we have given ourselves with positive, life-affirming ones, which can help our growth process. Anytime we are too critical or too harsh with ourselves, we only reinforce the very pattern we are attempting to eliminate. In order to move on we must forgive our past and ourselves for anything we wish we had done differently in our lives. No matter how often or hard we try, being harsh on ourselves will not change anything. Forgiveness, however, paves the way for new growth to form. It says to ourselves, "Okay, that's over and now

I can begin again." Without it, there is always a lingering part of our memory reminding us that we are not really capable of change.

Even though all types of inner work train us to become expectant of positive results, we must keep in mind that each of us will progress at our own rate. Our bodies will respond to our new way of thinking and our new self-image in their own time. For this reason it's important to set goals that are realistic. Ultimately, the most important part of your progress is not how much weight you are losing but rather that you notice how well you are doing at any given moment. For example, praising yourself when you demonstrate a positive result, such as turning down a second helping of food, passing up an offer of a beer, or losing even a single pound can be much more important and rewarding than a loss of ten pounds that goes virtually unrecognized. Each time you remind yourself, for whatever reason, that you are already doing well, you are reinforcing to yourself that you are capable of losing weight and, most importantly, are deserving of credit and a pat on the back.

Only through genuine forgiveness can we stop the endless cycle of guilt that most of us experience. We must forgive ourselves every time we think we are not doing well enough. It is our belief about not doing well enough that gives our subconscious minds the message that we are incapable of losing weight. Ultimately, the key to all successful living comes from a true inner love of ourselves. The way to achieve this self-love is through the process of forgiveness. Forgive yourself for not being good enough, for gaining weight, and for anything and everything you have ever done that makes you believe you are unworthy of love.

Most of us have a list a mile long of conditions we have placed on ourselves that we feel we must achieve before we would ever consider fully loving ourselves. For many, one of these conditions includes losing weight. As we release these conditions, and truly believe that we are deserving of love just the way we are, we will be giving our subconscious minds the life-affirming, positive message that we are capable of achieving anything we set our minds to.

There are three affirmations to practice for this chapter. Each of them is ideally suited to practice in a "practice period." If you recall from chapter 3, a practice period is a predetermined period of time (approximately five to ten minutes) during which you contemplate the affirmations you are practicing. Most of us are harder on ourselves than we might think. It's for this reason that "forgiveness" affirmations require a very deep commitment. Contemplating the specific words is an effective way to ingrain the messages into your subconscious mind.

The first affirmation for this chapter should be practiced often, with a great deal of love and meaning. Please repeat the message:

---

◆

# I FORGIVE MYSELF FOR ANY HARM I MAY HAVE CAUSED MYSELF

---

Say it again three times with love, conviction, and meaning!

---

◆

# I FORGIVE MYSELF FOR ANY HARM I MAY HAVE CAUSED MYSELF

◆

# I FORGIVE MYSELF FOR ANY HARM I MAY HAVE CAUSED MYSELF

◆

# I FORGIVE MYSELF FOR ANY HARM I MAY HAVE CAUSED MYSELF

---

The unforgiving mind is certain of its positions. It is incapable of seeing new possibilities because it is set in its ways. Because the unforgiving mind is so rigid in its belief system, it is incapable of change. How can a mind filled with judgment and condemnation allow the body to lose weight? Very simply, it can't. It's only through a true sense of forgiveness that we can appreciate ourselves enough to begin to take care of ourselves.

The next affirmation to practice reinforces the value of forgiveness in the process of losing weight. Again, a practice period can be very useful. It reads as follows:

---

## IT IS THROUGH MY FORGIVENESS THAT I WILL OBTAIN SUCCESS

---

Now try it again three times with a firm commitment that forgiveness is the key to success. Repeat the message with love and a genuine sense of meaning.

---

## IT IS THROUGH MY FORGIVENESS THAT I WILL OBTAIN SUCCESS

◆

## IT IS THROUGH MY FORGIVENESS THAT I WILL OBTAIN SUCCESS

◆

## IT IS THROUGH MY FORGIVENESS THAT I WILL OBTAIN SUCCESS

---

When we realize that it is only through forgiveness that we can love ourselves enough to achieve our goals, we will be on the road to achieving them. Forgiveness is the ultimate antidote to abusive criticism and negative thinking. It is only through forgiveness that we can let go of all our past misperceptions about ourselves that are keeping us from moving forward. Without it, the mind clings to its old idea of itself which includes aspects of negativity. As we let go of who we were through forgiveness, we pave the way to become who we wish to be.

Our final affirmation for this chapter is one of the most important in the entire book. Practice it often.

---

◆

IT IS THROUGH FORGIVENESS THAT I LOVE MYSELF; THE MORE I LOVE MYSELF, THE MORE I WILL CARE FOR MY BODY

---

As always, repeat the message many times with meaning, love, and commitment.

> IT IS THROUGH FORGIVENESS THAT I LOVE MYSELF; THE MORE I LOVE MYSELF, THE MORE I WILL CARE FOR MY BODY
>
> ◆
>
> IT IS THROUGH FORGIVENESS THAT I LOVE MYSELF; THE MORE I LOVE MYSELF, THE MORE I WILL CARE FOR MY BODY
>
> ◆
>
> IT IS THROUGH FORGIVENESS THAT I LOVE MYSELF; THE MORE I LOVE MYSELF, THE MORE I WILL CARE FOR MY BODY

If you are able to ingrain this ever-so-important message into your subconscious mind, you are on your way not only to a slimmer body but also toward a life of greater pleasure and inner joy. Forgiveness is the answer you need to erase any negative perceptions you have about yourself.

In addition to using affirmations for personal forgiveness, it's helpful to find additional exercises to work with. One of the most practical and effective exercises I've ever found is presented next.

## E X E R C I S E
# 19A

How many of us have actually taken the time to write ourselves a letter? Not many. The fact is, however, that writing yourself a letter is a wonderful way to communicate with, and learn about, the most important person in your life—you!

The procedure for this exercise is to write yourself a letter as if you were writing to your very best friend. The letter should be thoughtful and meaningful. The theme of the letter is, you guessed it, forgiveness.

Write yourself a very loving letter outlining the ways that you feel you need to forgive yourself. Think of periods of your life, specific instances, whatever it may be, that you feel need forgiving. Let yourself know that you love yourself just the way you are and for the way you have turned out to this point. No qualifications, no conditions, and no but-you-can-always-get-betters. Focus on the areas where you are usually hard on yourself. Find it in your heart to express to yourself genuine appreciation for your effort, accomplishment, and especially for your "being." Give yourself a pat on the back, and tell yourself that you are truly loving.

When you have completed the letter, read it slowly back to yourself out loud. Take in every word that you read. Allow yourself final freedom from your past. Allow yourself complete forgiveness. When you finish reading the letter, put it in a drawer. Refer to it at least three more times in the next week.

# Afterword

♦

I am convinced that the key to successful weight loss lies in the messages that are contained in our subconscious minds. We have seen throughout this book that we have been trained to give ourselves many negative messages that started in early childhood. These messages, if not looked at and consciously changed, can run our lives without our even knowing it. The secret to mastering our weight is to find the most effective means by which to connect with and alter the subconscious beliefs we have about ourselves. The best way to do this is through inner exercises such as relaxation, meditation, affirmations, visualization, breathing, and other creative exercises specifically designed to connect with the subconscious mind.

This book was designed and written to allow you to refer to it over and over again. While each message and chapter of the book is important in and of itself, my hope is that you will look at the book as a unitary whole. This means that each time you read the book, and/or practice the exercises contained in it, you will see the interconnectedness of the ideas.

The exercises contained in this book amount to a very necessary component of weight control—our attitudes and both our conscious and unconscious beliefs about eating, food, and our weight. With a genuinely positive mind-set anything is possible; without it, as we have seen, there is very little chance of success.

As you incorporate the messages and exercises in this book, you will sense how they can easily be transferred to other areas of your daily life. I encourage you to explore how inner work can enhance not only weight loss but virtually every other aspect of your life as well. Inner work has made a difference in my own life, in that of my clients, and for millions of others around the world. I know it can work for you. I wish you happiness, success, and love, and I thank you for reading this book.